MANAGING CONFLICT
God's Way

D1166961

MANAGING CONFLICT

CONFLICT

God's Way

DEBORAH
SMITH PEGUES

 Whitaker House

MANAGING CONFLICT—GOD'S WAY

For more information regarding tapes, seminars, or speaking engagements, write or call:
Deborah Smith Pegues
The Pegues Group
P.O. Box 78201
Los Angeles, CA 90016
(213) 293-5861
web site: www.wisdomcentral.com
e-mail: deborah@wisdomcentral.com

ISBN: 0-88368-516-7
Printed in the United States of America
Copyright © 1997 by Deborah Smith Pegues

Whitaker House
30 Hunt Valley Circle
New Kensington, PA 15068

Library of Congress Cataloging-in-Publication Data

Pegues, Deborah Smith, 1950–
        Managing conflict God's way / by Deborah Smith Pegues.
                p.   cm.
        Includes index.
        ISBN 0-88368-516-7 (trade paper : alk. paper)
        1. Conflict management—Religious aspects—Christianity. I. Title.
BV4597.53.C58P44 1997
248.4—dc21   97-43538

1 2 3 4 5 6 7 8 9 10 11 12 13 / 06 05 04 03 02 01 00 99 98 97

Quotes on *Managing Conflict—God's Way*

"We will experience conflict in our lives, but few of us know what to do about it. Some of us try to control situations with angry outbursts, and some ignore festering problems in hopes they will go away. In this book, Deborah Pegues shows us how to manage conflict in a practical way without offending others. We all need this book!"

Florence Littauer
Speaker/Author

"I appreciate the reminder that it is possible to confront without offending. Deborah Pegues deals with this subject with an authority that is the result of extensive study and research. At the same time, the book is very clear, easy to understand, and practical."

Bishop Charles E. Blake
General Board Member of the
International Churches of God in Christ

"There was a time when confrontation was not an option for me. I found it easier to look the other way. Now, I experience the freedom that only comes from confronting life's issues head-on. This book is informative, thought provoking, and packed with spiritual wisdom on a much needed subject."

Terry Cummings
NBA Star

Contents

Dedication

This book is dedicated to the memory of Dr. H. Marvin Smith and his wife, Dr. Juanita Smith, former pastors of the West Adams Foursquare Church of the Harvest in Los Angeles, California. As my spiritual mentors and cheerleaders, they were a model of generosity, faithfulness, forgiveness, and love. I am eternally grateful to God for allowing me the privilege of sitting under their ministry and witnessing real human saints firsthand.

Acknowledgments

Thanks to all of my family and friends who tolerated my unavailability as I attempted to obey God in completing this message to His people.

I am especially grateful to Harold and Ruth Kelley who encouraged me and shared their mountain retreat to create a perfect writing environment.

LaTonya Pegues's assistance went far beyond the call of duty.

My husband, Darnell Pegues, proved once again to be the most supportive and self-sufficient husband that any woman could ever desire.

Part I

Confrontation:
The Bridge to Harmony

Chapter One

The Goal of Confrontation

Problems and conflict are a fact of life. God did not create men and women to be carbon copies of each other. Therefore, in any relationship—personal, business, social, or spiritual—thorny issues will crop up that should be confronted. This book is designed to be a biblically based primer on how to confront these issues effectively.

The operative words here are *confront* and *effectively.* It has been my experience that most people, particularly Christians, are unwilling to confront at all. Those who do confront most often do so ineffectively.

Laree Kiely, Assistant Professor of Business Communications at the University of Southern California Business School, was quoted as saying the following in an article in the *Los Angeles Times,* "The problem is people have never really learned how to communicate with each other in straightforward ways without doing damage to their relationships, or [negotiate] their relationships so both have some room to change or some room to stay exactly the way they are."[1]

Confrontation can be the bridge between disharmony and harmony, between conflict and cooperation. Many shy away from it, but it is a powerful tool when done God's way.

The Lord provides the blessing at the place of unity: *"Behold, how good and how pleasant it is for brethren to dwell together in unity!...for there the* LORD *commanded the blessing, even life for evermore"* (Ps. 133:1, 3 KJV). The attempt to build the Tower of Babel was a vivid demonstration of the power of unity. After the Flood, God commanded the descendants of Noah to replenish the earth. They decided that they would build a city and stay in one place rather than disperse across the earth. They desired to build a tower that would reach into the heavens and serve as a memorial to themselves. They were unanimous in their opposition to God's will. Their plans would have succeeded if God had not intervened.

> But the LORD *came down to see the city and the tower that the men were building. The* LORD *said, "If as one people speaking the same language they have begun to do this, then nothing they plan to do will be impossible for them. Come, let us go down and confuse their language so they will not understand each other." So the* LORD *scattered them from there over all the earth, and they stopped building the city. That is why it was called Babel—because there the* LORD *confused the language of the whole world. From there the* LORD *scattered them over the face of the whole earth.* (Gen. 11:5–9 NIV)

Even God was impressed with the unity of those building the tower—though it was to serve an evil purpose.

The Goal of Confrontation

The interesting thing to note about this project is that, once they were unable to communicate, they were unable to build. If we cannot communicate, we cannot build anything. We cannot build a marriage; we cannot build a church; we cannot build a business.

To insure harmony, we must keep the doors of communication open. To do this, we must engage in effective confrontation when conflicts arise. The apostle Paul cautioned us to *"make every effort to keep the unity of the Spirit through the bond of peace"* (Eph. 4:3 NIV). He also admonished, *"If it is possible, as much as depends on you, live peaceably with all men"* (Rom. 12:18).

The challenge is clear. Each of us is to make it an active priority to stay in harmony with our fellowman. Harmony is not just a good concept that produces a pleasant environment. It creates synergy. The best way to explain synergy is to say that a hand is much more effective than five fingers working independently of each other. I tested this principle one day using dumbbells. I wanted to determine the maximum number of pounds that each of my fingers could lift independently. Two pounds was it. I then wanted to test the strength of my fingers working in unison, that is, as a hand. I rationalized that five fingers times two pounds each should yield a maximum of ten pounds. Not so. I lifted thirty-five pounds!

This is the concept referred to in Deuteronomy 32:30 when it speaks of one chasing a thousand and two putting ten thousand to flight. Logically, if one can impact a thousand, then two should only be able to impact two thousand. But such is the product of unity—we are ten times more effective when we join together. It is no wonder that Satan makes every attempt to keep us out of harmony. He knows that our togetherness will spell his doom.

CONFRONTING VERSUS RETALIATING

To begin to change our mind-set about confrontation, we need to understand its true definition. The word *confrontation,* like the word *diet,* has gotten a bad rap because of popular usage. Most of us associate diet with weight loss, hunger, and giving up one's favorite foods. However, a diet is simply any plan of eating. There are all kinds of diets, ranging from various types of health diets, to cosmetic diets that help to clear up skin problems, to weight loss diets. They are all diets.

And so it is with confrontation. We must therefore abandon any negative, preconceived ideas about confrontation and look at the true definition of the word. The prefix *con* means "together" or "with," and the root *fron* means "face; to stand or meet face-to-face." Confrontation is simply the act of coming together face-to-face to resolve an issue.

Many people want to know how my teaching here on confrontation can be reconciled to Jesus' teaching on turning the other cheek: *"To him who strikes you on the one cheek, offer the other also"* (Luke 6:29). In this passage, Jesus was admonishing the disciples to resist the urge to retaliate. The Lord wants us to be so positively against avenging the wrong that we would turn the other cheek. There is a vast difference between confrontation and retaliation.

The root meaning of *retaliation* is "to return the punishment." Suppose you and another person are dining at a restaurant, and the other person kicks you under the table several times. To retaliate would be to kick him back; to confront would be to say, "You may not be aware of it, but you are kicking my leg."

The Goal of Confrontation

DAVID VERSUS SAUL: CONFRONTING BUT NOT RETALIATING

He came to the sheep pens along the way; a cave was there, and Saul went in to relieve himself. David and his men were far back in the cave. The men said, "This is the day the LORD spoke of when he said to you, 'I will give your enemy into your hands for you to deal with as you wish.'" Then David crept up unnoticed and cut off a corner of Saul's robe. Afterward, David was conscience-stricken for having cut off a corner of his robe. He said to his men, "The LORD forbid that I should do such a thing to my master, the Lord's anointed, or lift my hand against him; for he is the anointed of the LORD." With these words David rebuked his men and did not allow them to attack Saul. And Saul left the cave and went his way. Then David went out of the cave and called out to Saul, "My lord the king!" When Saul looked behind him, David bowed down and prostrated himself with his face to the ground. He said to Saul, "Why do you listen when men say, 'David is bent on harming you'? This day you have seen with your own eyes how the LORD delivered you into my hands in the cave. Some urged me to kill you, but I spared you; I said, 'I will not lift my hand against my master, because he is the Lord's anointed.' See, my father, look at this piece of your robe in my hand! I cut off the corner of your robe but did not kill you. Now understand and recognize that I am not guilty of wrongdoing or rebellion. I have not wronged you, but you are hunting me down to take my life. May the LORD judge between you and me. And may the LORD avenge the wrongs you have done to me, but my hand will not touch you."   *(1 Sam. 24:3–12 NIV)*

David passed up a prime opportunity to avenge himself against King Saul's relentless pursuit to kill him for no apparent reason. Although he resisted the temptation to *retaliate,* he could not resist the need to *confront* him.

Giving him the benefit of the doubt, he sincerely wanted to know why King Saul had chosen to listen to those who had told him that David meant him harm. Frankly, it was not others who had inspired the king to his dire actions, but his own deep insecurity at hearing the women sing about David having killed tens of thousands of men versus Saul's thousands (1 Sam. 18:6–9). In the true fashion of a man after God's own heart, David never lost respect for the king's position of authority.

This is a good example to emulate if we ever have to confront someone in authority over us at church, at work, or at home. We must continue to respect and honor his or her position while seeking to gain an understanding and resolution of the problem—even when those around us are encouraging us to do otherwise.

It is God's will for us to confront. Jesus' communication was always clear and unequivocal. He did not talk out of both sides of His mouth, so to speak. Therefore, He meant what He said in Luke 17:3: *"Take heed to yourselves: If thy brother trespass against thee, rebuke him; and if he repent, forgive him"* (KJV). In the context of this verse, to rebuke simply means to tell him to stop. God wants us to deal with relational problems through such confrontation.

Chapter Two

When to Confront

As always, the answers to life's problems can be found in the Word of God. The Bible admonishes us to confront in three different situations: when we are offended, when we have offended, and when we observe a brother or sister behaving unwisely or in an ungodly manner. In all three instances, we are commanded to take the initiative in dealing with the issue. Let us look at these three instances and see what the Bible says about each of them.

WHEN WE ARE OFFENDED

In Matthew 18:15, Jesus said, *"Moreover if your brother sins against you, go and tell him his fault between you and him alone. If he hears you, you have gained your brother."* This is a clear admonition to confront the offender. In the subsequent verses, Jesus gave instructions on what to do if someone does not listen to you. That involves a group confrontation. In this book, however, I want to deal only with personal, individual confrontations.

Most Christians believe that it is a sign of humility and godliness to suffer silently when offended, hurt, or abused. Repressing your anger or frustration is unwise, though. Every repressed emotion gets expressed somewhere. Some people eat too much; others turn to alcohol or drugs. Still others may shop or become workaholics in order to work through the frustration of not confronting. All of these behaviors can be the result of repressed emotions. The medical profession has many documented cases of illnesses rooted in repressed emotions. I sat with a woman at a Christian women's luncheon not long ago who had suffered a stroke. When I asked her what had led to her stroke, she said that she had never spoken up when things bothered her.

Paul admonished us to watch out for the root of bitterness: *"Looking diligently lest any man fail of the grace of God; lest any root of bitterness springing up trouble you, and thereby many be defiled"* (Heb. 12:15 KJV).

The Holy Spirit has revealed to me that confrontation is the best safeguard against a root of bitterness. Bitterness is accumulated resentment. Resentment is unresolved anger that has been rerouted to our inner selves rather than dealt with through effective confrontation. In order for anything to take root, it must be underneath the surface. If not, it dies. We can kill resentment by not allowing it to go underground.

There are those who have such low boiling points or so much repressed anger and frustration that they explode at the slightest provocation. I call this the "simmer. and blow" syndrome. Obviously, this type of reaction does not fix the problem. Christians who carry these emotions around become dysfunctional before they know it. Now let me put your mind to rest regarding this psychological term that makes some of us uncomfortable. *Dysfunctional,* in layman's terms, simply means "not functioning or working according to its original purpose." Any dysfunctional behavior in us Christians is Satan's trap to keep us frustrated so that we cannot fulfill our divine purposes.

WHEN WE HAVE OFFENDED

Matthew 5:23–24 says,

Therefore if you bring your gift to the altar, and there remember that your brother has something against you, leave your gift there before the altar, and go your way. First be reconciled to your brother, and then come and offer your gift.

When we offend or become aware that we have offended another, it is our Christian responsibility to actively work toward a reconciliation. When we sense that someone has started to avoid us or we feel a strain in our relationship, it's time to take action. My husband and I often challenge each other to model our belief that the person who is more spiritually mature is always the one who initiates the reconciliation. Immature Christians wait for others to build bridges to them.

WHEN WE OBSERVE UNGODLY OR UNWISE BEHAVIOR

Our biblical text for the third instance of godly confrontation is found in Galatians 6:1: "*Brethren, if a man is overtaken in any trespass, you who are spiritual restore such a one in a spirit of gentleness, considering yourself lest you also be tempted.*"

Most Christians just pray or gossip when they see a brother or sister overtaken in a fault or other ungodly behavior. Few confront. Paul's admonition is directed to someone who is in a relationship with the one who needs to be confronted. Therefore, this passage is not a license for legalistic Christians to force their man-made rules onto naive new converts.

I have seen new converts totally turned off by the church because some unwise person confronted them about their outward appearance. Why not take the time to disciple new converts in the Word of God and to minister to their other needs first? In other words, earn the right to be heard. Once a Christian has established himself or herself as a godly, non-judgmental, and caring model, admonition may not even be necessary.

Regardless of one's Christian maturity, everyone is subject to falling into sin or, at least, into unwise behavior at some point in his Christian walk. Therefore, when we see a brother or sister straying from the godly path—whether in word or deed—it is our Christian obligation to *"restore such a one."* No one has twenty-twenty vision when looking at himself; we all have blind spots. It often takes someone with spiritual eyes to shine the light on our blindness.

Caution: Expect Defensiveness and Excuses

Not even the most humble person relishes the idea of having his faults, weaknesses, or shortcomings exposed. It is a natural response to become defensive or to justify our behavior. Defensiveness helps us to protect ourselves against the pain of the truth. Expect it, and don't be turned off by it. Job said, *"How painful are honest words!"* (Job 6:25 NIV). Many will either blame others for their actions or try to justify them. The biblical blamers include Eve, King Saul, Aaron, and countless others. Not everyone will respond as King David did, and say, *"I have sinned"* (2 Sam. 12:13).

Paul versus Peter: "Your Hypocrisy Is Hurting the Body!"

But when Peter was come to Antioch, I withstood him to the face, because he was to be blamed. For before that certain came from James, he did eat with the Gentiles: but when they were come, he withdrew and separated himself, fearing them which were of the circumcision. And the other Jews dissembled likewise with him; insomuch that Barnabas also was carried away with their dissimulation. But when I saw that they walked not uprightly according to the truth of the gospel, I said unto Peter before them all, If thou, being a Jew, livest after the manner of Gentiles, and not as do the Jews, why compellest thou the Gentiles to live as do the Jews?

(Gal. 2:11–14 KJV)

Here we have Peter, that anointed, Spirit-filled disciple, being a hypocrite. He felt that he needed to walk the tightrope between the Jewish Christians and the Gentile Christians. He had fellowshipped and dined freely with the Gentiles in Antioch, but then he chose to distance himself from them when the Jewish Christians came from Jerusalem. He did not wish to offend the Jews by eating with these uncircumcised Christians. Of course, the Gentiles were offended by his hypocrisy.

Paul knew that many followers emulate their leaders. Therefore, a leader walking in error must be confronted. Now some would suspect that Paul was probably jealous of Peter because of his status as an original disciple, but this was not so. Paul simply wanted to see Peter and the other leaders walk *"according to the truth of the gospel"* (v. 14). This Gospel declared that the circumcision laws were no longer in effect. There was now no difference between Jews and Gentiles. There was no need to prefer one group over the other.

It is interesting to note that even Barnabas, the anointed Jewish apostle to the Gentiles, was influenced by Peter's behavior and followed suit. Perhaps this was what led Paul to admonish us to confront any brother or sister overtaken in a fault. We are not to be intimidated by anyone's rank or background.

Paul's opposing Peter *"to the face"* (v. 11) is the best definition of a confrontation, that is, coming together face-to-face. Since Peter's offense was public, Paul publicly rebuked him. If public rebukes were practiced more today, we'd have fewer instances of ungodly leadership.

Peter's response to the rebuke is not revealed, but we can safely assume that he accepted it, for he was a lover of God's law. *"Great peace have they which love thy law: and nothing shall offend them"* (Ps. 119:165 KJV).

Part II

Biblical Confrontation and Conflict Management Styles

Introduction

Everyone uses a certain style or a combination of styles in dealing with various issues that arise. These styles range from the dictatorial, "do it my way," approach, to the low self-esteem, "we'll do it your way," approach. Have caution, though, because none of these styles is exclusively good or bad. The circumstances will dictate which style is the best in a given situation.

In this section, we will look at the various confrontation styles that biblical characters resorted to in the face of conflicts or disagreements, and I will show the lessons that we can learn from them. In a later chapter, we will also look at how one's basic personality style determines his behavior in a conflict.

Chapter Three

The Dictator

T here are some people who handle conflict through the following ways: charging, commanding, demanding, directing, imposing, mandating, ordering, proclaiming, ruling, calling the shots, and laying down the law. I call such people Dictators, and in this chapter I will discuss what makes up and contributes to the Dictator personality.

"DO IT MY WAY"

One of the signature songs of the legendary Frank Sinatra is the one in which he sings, "I did it my way." Now, I don't personally know whether or not Mr. Sinatra was a Dictator, but this song almost perfectly represents the Dictator's mind-set. The "my way" style of managing conflict does not succumb to or show regard for the opinions of others—especially when the person who uses this style of conflict management believes that he is right. A dissenting opinion is of no consequence to someone who resorts to this style, because the relationship with the offender is secondary to him.

Even though a smart leader or supervisor desires to have things done his way, he quickly realizes that there is more than one way to accomplish the same goal. The ability to be flexible is a character trait that can reap big dividends.

The Dictator engages in win-lose confrontations. He uses his power or anger to win at the expense of the other person. In many circumstances, this style reflects emotional and professional immaturity.

Some Dictators are in fact known to be confrontational in the popular sense of the word. They scream and yell, and they confront every perceived problem. They can be a real pain. You find yourself walking on eggshells around them, so to speak, for fear that you might offend them and set them off. I've seen managers in the workplace who resort to this type of behavior, and they don't engender any loyalty from their subordinates and are usually deeply resented. When we treat people with contempt and intimidation, we will not get the best from them. Proverbs 18:19 warns that *"a brother offended is harder to be won than a strong city: and their contentions are like the bars of a castle"* (KJV).

Use of the Dictator style is no way to motivate employees. Threatening subordinates with the loss of their jobs or lack of promotions and raises will only cause them to become mediocre and do just enough to stay employed.

THE DICTATOR SUPERVISOR

When I held a high-visibility position at a certain Fortune 500 company, I was adamant about the quality of the correspondence that went out of my department. Despite the fact that I had a superstar staff, I reviewed and made changes to all memos written by the staff in order to make them sound more like me. One day, because time was of the essence, I quickly reviewed a memo—in the presence of the writer—and concluded that it conveyed the message and required no grammatical corrections. Of course, I would have worded it differently, yet I simply stated that it was okay to send it. The woman who had written the memo was ecstatic. She said, "No changes? I can't believe it!" She was beaming. From that day forward, I made no changes or just minimal ones to staff memos. The impact on morale was amazing. I learned something that I had not learned in school: people need to feel that they exercise some control or authority in their environment. Does this mean that you become a compromising wimp? Heaven forbid, no! What it does mean is that you realize that by empowering those whom you have authority over, you build a loyal and creative winning team.

Nordstroms, the upscale department store, epitomizes the empowerment theory. The salesclerks are empowered to make exchange or refund decisions on the spot. They are rarely required to appeal to higher management. All of the them are extremely personable and seem to love their jobs. It's a pleasure to shop there. On the other hand, I know of a young Dictator pastor who is too insecure to allow his leaders to make even minor decisions without first consulting him, and he's rarely available. He will never build strong leaders. He will constantly be surrounded by yes-men whom he has trained by his own actions to show no initiative.

THE DICTATOR HUSBAND

The spiritually unwise husband who demands submission from his wife won't get it; he may get obedience, but not submission. Obedience is the performance of a requested action, but submission comes from the spirit. If my husband insists that I iron his underwear, I may resent the request but faithfully do the ironing. I may then consciously or unconsciously manifest my resentment in other areas of the marriage, much to his bewilderment. He wonders, "Why does she always have a headache when I want to be intimate?" With submission, on the other hand, a wife demonstrates the right spirit and attitude as she obeys. I believe that a man commands, that is, earns, submission by the way he treats his wife. No, I am not suggesting that wives demonstrate a bad attitude when they do not wish to submit. I consider myself a very submitted woman. My husband brags that I am! However, every day I am perfecting the art of confronting problematic issues as they arise, rather than allowing the root of bitterness to spring up and defile me.

JESUS CLEANSES THE TEMPLE: WHEN DICTATING IS BEST

Use of the Dictator style in managing conflict is sometimes the best option. When the law is at stake, when you know for sure that you are right, when a decision must be made and you're the only one who can make it, or when tough love must be practiced for the common good of all—then dictate! For example, if your drug-addicted child insists on bringing drugs into your home and creating a negative or threatening environment for others in the household, he must be clearly warned that his behavior will not be tolerated.

We see Jesus resorting to this style when He cleansed the temple in Jerusalem:

And they come to Jerusalem: and Jesus went into the temple, and began to cast out them that sold and bought

in the temple, and overthrew the tables of the money-changers, and the seats of them that sold doves; and would not suffer that any man should carry any vessel through the temple. And he taught, saying unto them, Is it not written, My house shall be called of all nations the house of prayer? but ye have made it a den of thieves.
(Mark 11:15–17 KJV)

Jesus was on the warpath for the common good. He could not afford to allow the merchants to desecrate the worship environment with their commercial activity. To have kept silent would have set a precedent that would ultimately have resulted in the deterioration of the temple. Compromising was out of the question.

My husband, Darnell, and I often host family and other gatherings in our home. As you would expect, not all of our guests or family members are Christians. Now, Darnell is a very principled man and very adamant about maintaining the sanctity of our home. The general house rule of conduct is that no activity can be engaged in that would displease God, that is, no profanity, worldly music, drinking, or smoking. Several have been turned off by his refusal to compromise. I highly respect him for his stand. Many Christians are afraid to let their standards be made known; they are afraid that they might offend someone, or they do not wish to be labeled as "Holy Joes."

DICTATORS HAVE NEEDS, TOO!

I'm from a large family. As the one who is normally in charge of arranging all family functions, I generally plan all gatherings and celebrations. Several years ago, my husband and I moved into a new house around the same time as my birthday. We were so exhausted from all of the unpacking that we couldn't bring ourselves to plan a special celebration. On the Sunday afternoon of my birthday, a certain married couple dropped by to say hello. While they were there, my brother came over with his five-year-old daughter, Ashley, to wish me happy birthday. Of all of my six brothers who live in the Los Angeles area, only one had remembered my birthday. We were all sitting on the patio, when I excused myself to go and make punch for everyone. Ashley followed me into the kitchen. She came over, leaned her head against me, and very sympathetically stated, "Auntie Deborah, I feel so sorry for you that only four people came to your birthday party."

Now Ashley was used to big birthday parties where not only all of her friends were invited, but also her whole family from both her mother's and her father's sides. So I quickly corrected her, "Oh no, sweetheart, this isn't a party. The couple just stopped by."

She took a long look at me and said, "But you gotta feel bad, 'cause there aren't enough people here to have any fun with!"

Okay, Okay. So I felt bad that the others hadn't remembered. Ashley was not letting me stay in denial on this one. Later, I told my family that I was really disappointed that they hadn't remembered. They made up for it the next year. Ashley, who has the memory of an elephant, said that she still wasn't impressed with the number of people at that party either.

Sometimes it's pretty hard for Dictators to express their needs to others. They try to stay in control of their vulnerabilities. Consequently, others assume that Dictators need nothing and treat them accordingly. Yes, I'm often a Dictator, and in this example from my own life, it is possible to see how my needs were not expressed properly. If they had been, my family probably would have been more conscientious about celebrating my birthday that year. If you're a Dictator, spare yourself some pain, and let others know that you have needs, too.

YOUR CHALLENGE

Are there any situations where you need to practice the Dictator style because moral values are at stake or the common good is being threatened? Are there any situations where you need to stop practicing this style and to start focusing on hearing and valuing the input of others? Why not solicit a close, spiritual friend to monitor you in this area? Give him or her permission to offer you objective feedback on your behavior.

Chapter Four

The Accommodator

In contrast to the Dictator personality, some people handle conflict by always accommodating to the needs and wants of others. Such people do so through the following ways: adapting, adjusting, conforming, gratifying, indulging, obliging, pleasing, serving, and favoring. In this chapter, I will explain the style of the Accommodator.

"HAVE IT YOUR WAY"

Burger King, the popular fast-food franchise, has a slogan with which we should all be familiar: "Have it your way." Unlike McDonald's, with its standard lettuce, pickles, ketchup, and all-beef hamburger patties, Burger King promises to cater to our individual preferences. Burger King aims to please so that the restaurant chain may obtain and maintain our patronage. Loss of this patron relationship is the restaurant's great fear. The obvious thinking is that if we please you, you'll prefer us; if we do not please you, you'll abandon us for the competition. Ironically, Burger King is not the winner in the fast-food franchise war—and you won't be a winner either in the game of life if you are always seeking to please others. This is the lifestyle of the Accommodator.

To accommodate means to adapt or conform to new conditions, to oblige or cater to the needs of another. Accommodation is behavior that we learned in childhood. Little girls in particular are socialized at an early age to please others. One of my great pastimes is playing with children. Often, I've heard little girls at play threaten a non-complying playmate with a warning such as, "I'm not going to be your friend." The alienated victim learns that not pleasing others affects the quality of her life—her play-time—and may have negative consequences. So she learns to comply with their wishes.

The "have it your way" mind-set of the Accommodator is codependency at its worst. The fear of rejection, alienation, or abandonment is so great that confrontation is out of the question. The Accommodator wants to maintain the relationship at any cost, even at the cost of his own beliefs and values, peace of mind, personal time, or resources. He has low self-esteem and thus does not feel that he brings anything of real value to any relationship. Therefore, he goes to great lengths to be accepted by catering to the desires of others. The risk of confrontation is too great; acceptance is king!

Many Christians feel that to suffer in silence is their laudable duty. After all, they rationalize, Jesus suffered on the cross and never said a mumbling word! They'd rather keep quiet for the sake of having peace. They have defined peace as the absence of conflict or argument.

The Accommodator

My friend, when you are fuming, fretting, and experiencing other forms of inner turmoil, you have not kept the peace. Yes, you have avoided an argument, but you have created an internal storm. Real peace must be on the inside, and it comes through effective confrontation.

THE ACCOMMODATOR PARENT

I have observed many guilt-ridden single parents who refuse to discipline a disobedient or wayward child for fear that he will shift his love and affection to the other, non-resident, parent. The child, who is always seeking limits or boundaries for his behavior, never finds any from such a parent. Sally P. is a single parent raising two teenage daughters who demonstrate no respect for her. She sacrifices much for them. They see their father on weekends, and he's the good guy. The father seems to have the girls' respect already, whereas the mother is always afraid of losing it and therefore has very little. I have gleaned from our conversations that she fears the alienation of their affection; therefore, she lets them have everything their way. Ironically, this self-sacrificing desire for love and acceptance never comes to fruition. In fact, the opposite results occur. No one respects a wimp!

THE ACCOMMODATOR SUPERVISOR

I have also noticed in the workplace that a supervisor will often ignore an employee's negative behavior or performance for fear of the unpleasantness of a confrontation. This creates a mediocre staff and demoralizes would-be superstars.

Accommodator supervisors will often develop new rules and mandates that influence, inconvenience, or demoralize everybody, when in fact they are catered toward one person whom the supervisor refuses to confront. I can assure you that your staff will lose respect for you as their leader if you don't deal with problematic situations in a timely and mature manner.

Furthermore, as a supervisor or manager, you are responsible for developing the skills and working relationships of your employees; avoiding a confrontation is a bad example to set. Furthermore, unresolved problems distract you as well as your workers and hinder all from focusing on performance and meeting company objectives. Everybody loses. Once you establish a reputation for being able to confront and work through thorny issues, you'll gain the respect of your superiors, your peers, and your employees or staff.

I'm reminded of my three-year stint with a large aerospace company in southern California. When I took a high-profile management position, my subordinates had more experience than I and were all of a different ethnicity to boot. I decided that rather than be intimidated by these realities, I would conduct myself as the manager the company expected me to be.

I extolled the virtues of effective confrontation from the very beginning. I admonished the staff to attempt to resolve their conflicts and issues among themselves before presenting a certain situation to me. I also encouraged them to confront me without fear of repercussion; I applauded them when they did. I must confess that I never enjoyed being confronted, but I always experienced growth. Even after I left the company, I had former staff members come to my home and rehearse confrontations they were planning to have with a manager or peer. It was a very challenging and professionally rewarding experience.

The Accommodator

ABRAM AND LOT: PEACE AT ANY COST

The story of Abram and Lot tells us more about the Accommodator, and it is one example of when accommodating is the right thing to do.

> *Now Lot, who was moving about with Abram, also had flocks and herds and tents. But the land could not support them while they stayed together, for their possessions were so great that they were not able to stay together. And quarreling arose between Abram's herdsmen and the herdsmen of Lot. The Canaanites and Perizzites were also living in the land at that time. So Abram said to Lot, "Let's not have any quarreling between you and me, or between your herdsmen and mine, for we are brothers. Is not the whole land before you? Let's part company. If you go to the left, I'll go to the right; if you go to the right, I'll go to the left." Lot looked up and saw that the whole plain of the Jordan was well watered, like the garden of the LORD, like the land of Egypt, toward Zoar. (This was before the LORD destroyed Sodom and Gomorrah.) So Lot chose for himself the whole plain of the Jordan and set out toward the east. The two men parted company.   (Gen. 13:5–11 NIV)*

How can one not love a guy like Abram? His generosity and his desire to avoid strife are endearing. He and his nephew, Lot, had probably come through many toils and trials together since leaving their homeland, but even though they had, the relationship remained intact. Oddly enough, Lot was not mentioned in God's great promise to the Patriarch; God had blessed him simply because he was with Abram. Now the prosperity separated them.

Lot appeared to be a real taker! Abram so valued their relationship that he gave him first choice of the land. You'd think that Lot would be so grateful to this loving senior citizen who had caused him to be blessed, that he would take the least desirable real estate. But no, he chose the well-watered plains of Jordan. Such a self-centered act would be enough to start a root of bitterness in most of us. But Abram was able to avoid such bitterness.

Prosperity can separate the closest of kin. Just let Aunt Suzie or Uncle Joe pass away without a will and leave behind an extra dollar or two. Family members who have had a long history together will part company in the fight to get the largest share. Abram is an example for us because he did not have a scarcity mentality. The scarcity mentality says, "There is only enough for me to be blessed. I will be disadvantaged if I share the blessing—or the glory or the information or the recipe or the how-tos—with you." Steven Covey, in his book *The Seven Habits of Highly Effective People,* explains that people with a scarcity mentality "see life as having only so much, as though there were only one pie out there. And if someone were to get a big piece of the pie, it would mean less for everybody else."[2] This mind-set is played out each day in businesses, in the administration of the church, and in families around the world.

But Abram knew God. He knew that he would get what was promised to him. Maintaining the relationship with Lot was more important than owning prime real estate. And through the surety of God's Word, we find that God reaffirmed His promises to Abram as soon as Lot departed.

> *The LORD said to Abram after Lot had parted from him, "Lift up your eyes from where you are and look north and south, east and west. All the land that you see I will give to you and your offspring forever."* (Gen. 13:14–15 NIV)

AARON VERSUS THE MULTITUDE: THE ELOQUENT ACCOMMODATOR

The desire to please is not a modern-day phenomenon. When God charged Moses to lead the Israelites out of

Egypt, Moses complained that he was inadequate for the job because he was not eloquent. God assuaged his fears by allowing Aaron to be Moses' spokesperson since Aaron was indeed eloquent.

In Exodus 32, the children of Israel had been delivered out of Egypt and were en route to the Promised Land. When God summoned Moses to Mount Sinai to give him the Law, Moses left Aaron in charge of the multitude. After Moses had been gone for forty days and nights, the Israelites became restless and impatient with his absence. And now we find that this man-pleasing spirit dominated Aaron's leadership style and yielded dire results:

> *When the people saw that Moses was so long in coming down from the mountain, they gathered around Aaron and said, "Come, make us gods who will go before us. As for this fellow Moses who brought us up out of Egypt, we don't know what has happened to him." Aaron answered them, "Take off the gold earrings that your wives, your sons and your daughters are wearing, and bring them to me." So all the people took off their earrings and brought them to Aaron. He took what they handed him and made it into an idol cast in the shape of a calf, fashioning it with a tool. Then they said, "These are your gods, O Israel, who brought you up out of Egypt." When Aaron saw this, he built an altar in front of the calf and announced, "Tomorrow there will be a festival to the LORD." (Exod. 32:1–5 NIV)*

Notice that Aaron did not protest or offer any resistance to their sinful request. He did not wish to be unpopular.

Moses returned and confronted Aaron about what he had done. Moses knew that Aaron had been influenced by the people. Thus, he asked, *"What did these people do to you, that you led them into such great sin?"* (Exod. 32:21

NIV). Aaron, fearing Moses' anger and feeling caught between a rock and a hard place, responded, *"Do not be angry, my lord....You know how prone these people are to evil"* (v. 22 NIV).

As a result of Aaron's allowing the Israelites to "have it their way," three thousand people died that day. The moral of this story is that by not standing firm and by not exercising tough love we often cause the figurative death of others and sometimes ourselves. Let me explain what I mean. Death is separation. The Accommodator often causes some to be separated from lessons of life that they could have learned or some to forfeit benefits that they could have had, such as emotional and spiritual development, financial responsibility, personal independence, and even eternal life, to name a few. One of the most tragic Scriptures in the Bible is found in John 12:

> *Nevertheless among the chief rulers also many believed on him; but because of the Pharisees they did not confess him, lest they should be put out of the synagogue: for they loved the praise of men more than the praise of God.*   *(John 12:42–43 KJV)*

These leaders chose to forfeit eternal riches rather than to risk alienation from the synagogue!

The good news is that God does not hate or refuse to use Accommodators. For even while Aaron was making the golden calf, God was making plans for him to become the high priest. In Exodus 28:2, God instructed Moses to *"make holy garments for Aaron your brother, for glory and for beauty."* A few chapters later, Aaron had made the golden calf. God is not shocked by our humanity; He remembers that we are just dust. God knows that He has put in each of us the potential to be what He wants us to be. He focuses on what we will be, not on what we are.

The Accommodator

HOW TO STOP BEING AN ACCOMMODATOR

I offer the following guidelines to let go of this destructive Accommodator behavior.

See Everyone on the Same Plane

Most people with low self-esteem view others in some form of a hierarchy. All of the educated, beautiful, thin, wealthy, popular folks, or those in positions of authority, are at the top; the Accommodator sees himself on the bottom. He considers himself privileged when he finds himself in the company of such people. It is his honor to serve such worthy ones. He would never offend one of these people by saying no to any request, no matter how inconvenienced he may be in performing it.

Now God is not a respecter of people's social standings; that is, He does not esteem one human being higher than another. He loves and views all men the same. In my attempt to become more like Him, I conscientiously refuse to exalt one person above another, and I certainly refuse to exalt anyone above myself.

During the course of my work as a CPA and financial consultant, I often interact with wealthy people, heads of well-known organizations, or other well-known individuals. While I respect their positions, achievements, and contributions to society, I do not esteem them more highly than any other ordinary people with whom I interact on a regular basis. On a trip to South Africa, I was looking forward with great anticipation to meeting Winnie Mandela. When it appeared that such a meeting was subject to terms that I found too troublesome, I abandoned the idea without hesitation and immediately shifted my enthusiasm to an upcoming visit to the shanty towns where the disenfranchised black majority resides. I know that such an attitude is a work of God's grace, and I am a grateful, delivered Accommodator.

Express Your Boundaries

In real estate, every piece of property has property lines that let us know the domain of the owner. Anyone who crosses the line without the owner's permission is a trespasser. Because an Accommodator often fails to express or clarify his property lines or boundaries, people are constantly trespassing on his rights. When I first started teaching the concept of setting boundaries, I used to say that some people had no boundaries; however, as I interacted with more Accommodators, I came to realize that we all have limits beyond which we would prefer others not go. It's just that some people are hesitant to express these boundaries.

I know a tenderhearted Christian woman who is always ready to minister to any need that is presented to her. God has especially anointed her to pray for the sick and to encourage the distraught. The problem is that she does not express any of her own boundaries. People call her at all times of the night. They engage her in extremely long conversations and counseling sessions. She complains to her family about these intrusions but has never put a stop to them. Knowing that she would never refuse to counsel or minister to anyone, her daughter purchased an answering machine for her, but she rarely uses it. She'd rather continue to complain and allow her health to deteriorate from lack of rest than to risk possible alienation by those who take advantage of her lack of boundaries.

I heard someone say that the first time someone uses you, shame on them. The second time, shame on you! I am a firm believer that you teach people how to treat you by what you tolerate. Yes, settle this thought in your spirit, and repeat it often: "I teach people how to treat me by what I tolerate."

For over a year I ran my accounting practice from my home. Because most of my clients knew I worked out of the house, many would call at irregular hours and on weekends. Finally, frustrated by their insensitivity to my personal life, I left a recorded message that stated. "This phone is only answered Monday through Friday from 8:30 A.M. to 6:30 P.M." I realized that by answering the phone at odd hours, I had taught my clients that it was okay to call anytime. The moral of this story is, Do not create any monsters you don't plan to feed.

Or consider this situation of a new acquaintance who called me too early in the mornings. She was calling to encourage me to stay focused on writing this book. One day I said to her, "I really appreciate your calling to encourage me in writing the book. You'd probably like to know that I don't get up before 7:30 A.M. I really do need the motivation, so please feel free to call me after that time." *A boundary was set.*

How do you feel about people who show up at your house without calling first? If it really bothers you, you need to advise the offender the very first time that it happens that you would prefer advance notice: "Sally, it is so nice to see you. Please call before you come next time so that I can block some quality time for our visit." *A boundary is set.*

The following letter appeared in the "Dear Abby" column on October 23, 1994, in the *Los Angeles Times:*

Dear Abby:

My younger brother is currently serving a one-year sentence in a federal prison. When he telephones me, he must call collect because this is the rule. At first I was glad to hear from him, but frankly, I simply cannot afford to accept all these calls. I write to him often, but he calls several times a week to chat. Abby, I know he is lonely, but my husband's patience is growing thin—and I don't blame him. Our telephone bills are more than we can handle. In addition to those phone bills, he asks me to send him money for postage stamps, toiletries, and money to pay his court fines. I hate to hurt his feelings, but this has got to stop. Why does the prison system allow inmates to make unlimited collect calls? Surely the prison administrators realize the burden it places on family members.

Signed,
"Had It In Arkansas"

Abby responded:

Dear "Had It":

Tell your brother you will accept only one collect call a month, and if he calls more than that, you will refuse his call. Also, send him no money unless you can easily afford it.

I applaud Abby's response; it is very similar to the one I would have given. This woman simply needed to set some boundaries. I offer the following script for the confrontation with the brother: "Mark, I sympathize with your plight in being incarcerated. I'm sure that this must be a trying experience. Because my family and I must live within a limited budget, I'm going to have to restrict our phone conversations to once each month. Let me know which day of the month you plan to call so that we can be sure to be home. I will attempt to write to you as often as I can. Also, as our budget allows, I will send you some money for stamps and so forth. We look forward to your release." *Boundaries have been set!*

The Accommodator

JESUS AND THE RICH YOUNG RULER: BOUNDARIES WITH CONSEQUENCES

The following example from Scripture shows that setting boundaries must have consequences:

> *And a certain ruler asked him, saying, Good Master, what shall I do to inherit eternal life? And Jesus said unto him, Why callest thou me good? none is good, save one, that is, God. Thou knowest the commandments, Do not commit adultery, Do not kill, Do not steal, Do not bear false witness, Honour thy father and thy mother. And he said, All these have I kept from my youth up. Now when Jesus heard these things, he said unto him, Yet lackest thou one thing: sell all that thou hast, and distribute unto the poor, and thou shalt have treasure in heaven: and come, follow me. And when he heard this, he was very sorrowful: for he was very rich. And when Jesus saw that he was very sorrowful, he said, How hardly shall they that have riches enter into the kingdom of God!* (Luke 18:18–24 KJV)

Jesus was sorrowful because He knew that the young man had made a bad decision and that He could not compromise the requirements. Because riches had such a hold on him, Jesus didn't just ask him to pay tithes or to give offerings; He wanted him to forsake all. Before we criticize the ruler, let's take a moment to appreciate some aspects of his character. He was one in authority who had high moral values. Unlike a lot of today's leaders, he hadn't been associated with scandals and corruption. He felt that he had kept all of the commandments from his youth. He cared about his spiritual life and his eternal destiny. He did not share the fear of the other rulers of that day who wouldn't confess the Lord for fear that they would be put out of the synagogue (John 12:42). Following Jesus was not the popular thing to do, yet he was willing to suffer the alienation and the rejection of his peers. He simply had this one all-consuming attachment—his riches. And, because Jesus wouldn't negotiate, he was going to have to forfeit eternal life!

Now, imagine the state of Christianity had Jesus been willing to compromise. We would all be trying to negotiate one little pet vice to hold on to. "Jesus, I'll do everything else you require, just let me keep my mistress, my gambling habit, or my bitterness."

What about you? How firm are your boundaries? Do you often say "yes" when you really want to say "no"? Do others take liberties with your possessions? Please be warned that Accommodators are prone to developing a root of bitterness. They dislike themselves and experience low self-esteem for not being true to their own desires and wishes.

Consciously Value Your Intangible Assets

In accounting, there are two types of assets: tangible and intangible. The tangible assets have physical substance, that is, they can be seen and touched; thus their values can be objectively determined by a qualified appraiser based on his observations. Buildings, vehicles, furniture, equipment, and so forth fall into this category.

The intangible assets present a more interesting valuation dilemma in that they have no physical substance; their value is derived from the rights or other future benefits they represent for the owner. The goodwill of a business is a typical example. Its value cannot be seen, but it is present. Let me explain this through the following example.

Many times when someone purchases an existing business, he will pay more for the business than the tangible assets are worth. For example, assume that Mr. X desires to purchase a local restaurant. The building and equipment are appraised at $300,000; however, Mr. X is willing to pay $700,000 for the restaurant because it has been in business for over twenty years, owns unique recipes, and is a favorite gathering place throughout the region. He is willing to pay an extra $400,000 for this inherent *goodwill*. Mr. X has placed more value on the intangible than the tangible.

In today's society, we are constantly bombarded with media messages that put the emphasis on the physical, and Christians have bought into the system. We put more value on physical beauty, possessions, and other temporal tangibles than such eternal intangibles as integrity, kindness, patience, impartiality, and faithfulness, to name a few. I challenge you to be a maverick and stop this madness!

Start right now. Make a list of your God-given intangibles. Meditate on each one, and give it a high value. Here's a list of mine to get you started:

- In my social life, I don't discriminate between the haves and the have nots.

- I have a good understanding of the Bible.

- I love giving sacrificially and encouraging others to do so.

- I am always optimistic.

- I have a good sense of humor.

- I inspire and motivate anyone who wants to accomplish a goal.

- I am objective and unbiased; therefore, I am good at resolving conflict.

- I have very clear boundaries.

Stop now, and take this opportunity to make your own list.

My intangible assets:

_____

_____

_____

_____

_____

Now, the world may not put as much stock in the above as we do, but remember, these assets are priceless. So, next time you're tempted to exalt someone else's tangibles, review your list, and thank God for His wonderful gifts to you.

WHEN ACCOMMODATING IS BEST

Before we conclude that accommodating is always bad, let me caution that this can sometimes be the best option. Such would be the case in the following instances:

- You have prayerfully concluded that you'd rather maintain the relationship as is than risk the possible consequences of a confrontation. This is related to how Abram dealt with Lot in the example given earlier in the chapter.

- You realize that you are fighting city hall, so to speak, and probably will not prevail. This is especially true when the other person is refusing to acknowledge his or her blind spot.

- You have decided to allow the other person to experience the law of sowing and reaping, so that he may learn a lesson. God did this with the children of Israel: *"And he gave them their request; but sent leanness into their soul"* (Ps. 106:15 KJV).

YOUR CHALLENGE

Consider some areas in your current relationships in which you are unconsciously or unintentionally teaching others that their wrong behavior toward you is okay. Ask God for a creative way to put an end to it. Then set a deadline for doing so.

Also, as you begin to set boundaries, be careful not to go overboard and build a wall. It is Satan's strategy to have us go from one extreme to the other. Walls keep people out of our lives; this is not God's will. Boundaries are like fences with gates; we can allow entrance to others as we deem wise and appropriate. Thus, boundaries are meant to help others to know how far they can go into our territory.

Chapter Five

The Abdicator

Another way of handling conflict is embodied by the type of person whom I will call the Abdicator. Someone like this handles conflict through the following ways: retreating, bowing out, quitting, stepping down, separating himself or herself, dropping out, walking away, and abandoning.

To abdicate is to relinquish power or responsibility. Renowned psychologist, M. Scott Peck, asserts in his book, *The Road Less Traveled,* that "the tendency to avoid problems...is the primary cause of all mental illness."[3] If this is true, then the Abdicator would be a prime candidate for a mental disorder.

The Abdicator avoids confrontation at any cost. He would rather leave the environment, or withdraw from a situation, than confront. He refuses to experience the growth that results from working through issues.

The Abdicator leaves the church when he is offended and doesn't tell anybody why. He makes no attempt to try to understand the motive or intentions of the one who has offended him. He fails to realize that many times the person who offended him may be totally unaware that he did so and meant no ill will. If he hadn't run away, he would have found out.

The Abdicator will often quit a job with little or no notice. Once I had a friend over for dinner who related the story of how she had been working with a nonprofit organization and had become quite perturbed at how the director was running the program. One day she just quit, leaving her boss high and dry. The director was appalled at such short notice and begged her to tell her what prompted her to quit. She related to me that she never gave the woman an explanation. How unfortunate, irresponsible, and unprofessional. What was the worst that could have happened if she had confronted the director early on? Perhaps she would have been fired. I doubt it.

Pouting is another example of an abdicator's behavior. The pouting wife retreats to silence, leaving her husband guessing as to what is bothering her rather than expressing her frustration in a spiritually mature way. Of course, men are guilty of this behavior, also. No one should expect anyone to be a mind reader. Express what you need. Don't waste time being upset that he or she *should* know. In fact, don't assume anything. When I speak to married couples, I admonish men and women alike to move from Shouldsville. Ask for what you want. If his opening your car door is important to you—men, it's important to all of us!—then tell him that it would really make you happy if he did it. Don't resort to this passive-aggressive behavior. The silence is passive while the purpose behind it is aggressive and is striking out. Passive-aggressive behavior is against the will of God. Matthew 18:15 clearly admonishes us to *"go and tell"* the offender his fault.

I believe that a man who always succumbs to the silent treatment, by begging his wife to tell him why she's pouting, teaches the woman that this is an effective way to get his attention. Remember that you teach by what you tolerate.

I've noticed when playing with small children that one of them, usually a girl, will often pout and withdraw from the rest if things aren't going her way. I have always admonished the other children to ignore the pouter. I can't afford to teach the pouter that her behavior will get results. Eventually, she comes out of it and joins us.

THE PRODIGAL'S BROTHER:
AN ABDICATOR'S RESENTMENT

Luke 15 relates the story of the Prodigal Son, who squandered his inheritance on worldly living. After hitting rock bottom, he decided to repent and go home to his father where he could live well again. His father, delighted that his son had come to his senses, threw a party upon his arrival. The sensible, older son, who had never left his father and had served him well, was quite upset by the celebration:

> *Now his elder son was in the field: and as he came and drew nigh to the house, he heard music and dancing. And he called one of the servants, and asked what these things meant. And he said unto him, Thy brother is come; and thy father hath killed the fatted calf, because*

he hath received him safe and sound. And he was angry,
and would not go in: therefore came his father out, and
entreated him.   *(Luke 15:25–28 KJV)*

The father was obviously a wise man and a Collaborator, which I will discuss in the next chapter. Many times
we have to initiate contact and reach out to Abdicators—at
least once—to give them the opportunity to explain their
pain or frustration.

And he answering said to his father, Lo, these many
years do I serve thee, neither transgressed I at any time
thy commandment: and yet thou never gavest me a kid,
that I might make merry with my friends: but as soon
as this thy son was come, which hath devoured thy liv-
ing with harlots, thou hast killed for him the fatted
calf. And he said unto him, Son, thou art ever with me,
and all that I have is thine. It was meet that we should
make merry, and be glad: for this thy brother was
dead, and is alive again; and was lost, and is found.
               (vv. 29–32)

Although the son expressed that he felt unappreciated, the father didn't cater to his erroneous assessment
of this situation by canceling the party. He simply explained to him that having the celebration was the right
thing to do.

One should not cater to an Abdicator just to retain a
relationship. Doing so creates an imbalance that will ultimately destroy the relationship anyway. For instance, we
should not allow a person or group who is out of fellowship or at odds with someone to dictate what our relationship with that person should be. When I was in college,
my roommate and I pledged rival sororities. My new so-
rority sisters were often perturbed that I continued my

relationship with my roommate and that I often visited the enemy camp. I choose to believe that my interests are quite broad. In fact, they are broad enough to allow me to socialize with an alienated party and to engage in conversations that do not focus on the issues that divide him or her from my other friends. In fact, I am in a better position to build a bridge of reconciliation when I have access to both sides.

We should be careful not to put this kind of pressure on anyone to choose sides just because we haven't been able to, or because we refuse to, be reconciled to someone. This is ungodly behavior.

ABRAM, SARAI, AND HAGAR: THE ACCOMMODATOR, THE DICTATOR, AND THE ABDICATOR

Now Sarai Abram's wife bare him no children: and she had an handmaid, an Egyptian, whose name was Hagar. And Sarai said unto Abram, Behold now, the LORD hath restrained me from bearing: I pray thee, go in unto my maid; it may be that I may obtain children by her. And Abram hearkened to the voice of Sarai. And Sarai Abram's wife took Hagar her maid the Egyptian, after Abram had dwelt ten years in the land of Canaan, and gave her to her husband Abram to be his wife. And he went in unto Hagar, and she conceived: and when she saw that she had conceived, her mistress was despised in her eyes. And Sarai said unto Abram, My wrong be upon thee: I have given my maid into thy bosom; and when she saw that she had conceived, I was despised in her eyes: the LORD judge between me and thee. But Abram said unto Sarai, Behold, thy maid is in thy hand; do to her as it pleaseth thee. And when Sarai dealt hardly with her, she fled from her face. And the angel of the LORD found her by a fountain of water in the wilderness, by the fountain in the way to Shur. And he said, Hagar, Sarai's maid, whence camest thou? and

*whither wilt thou go? And she said, I flee from the face
of my mistress Sarai. And the angel of the LORD said
unto her, Return to thy mistress, and submit thyself under her hands.*   *(Gen. 16:1–9 KJV)*

Sarai had waited long enough. Perhaps she and Abram
had misinterpreted God's promise. It was time to take
matters into her own hands. The root meaning of *Sarai* is
"ruler, captain, or governor." True to her name, Sarai began to dictate what course of action she and Abram should
take. Later, God changed her name to Sarah, which means
"lady or princess," for she had learned to stop dictating to
her husband. But first, she commanded Abram to sleep
with her maid, Hagar. Being the Accommodator that he
was, he consented.

After becoming pregnant, Hagar developed a poor attitude toward Sarai and began to despise her. Big mistake!
One should be careful about offending a Dictator who has
authority over him or her. In characteristic dictator style,
Sarai responded decisively and without consideration for
Hagar's feelings. Sarai scolded her severely, forcing her to
run away.

Having no apparent financial options and no emotional
or other support from Abram (Mr. Burger King), one would
think that Hagar would have humbled herself, repented of
her insolent attitude, and begged Sarai's forgiveness. But
no! Abdicators relinquish all power and responsibility for
making a difference in their situations. So she fled. In fact,
Hagar means "flight." She was acting out her true nature.
Notwithstanding, she probably felt that a discussion with
Sarai would be futile. Most people fear a direct confrontation with a Dictator.

Surely, Hagar, as the maid, had other responsibilities to
the household. She did not stop to consider how abandoning

such duties would impact anyone else. She wanted to get out of there! The angel of the Lord instructed her to *"return"* and to *"submit"* to Sarai (Gen. 16:9). So she tucked her tail, swallowed her pride, and went back home.

The lessons we should learn from Hagar are threefold. First, we should learn to remain humble when God blesses us or raises us up to an advantageous position. Secondly, we need to put the blame on ourselves when we are cast out because of our pride. And thirdly, we need to know that even when we mess up, God is still faithful to His divine plan.

WHEN ABDICATING IS GOOD

Abdicating or retreating is not always bad if it is temporary. Sometimes we need to pull back to allow ourselves to respond rationally and in accordance with the will of God. We often need to seek His guidance and to get in touch with our own emotions. Other times, we may realize that we do not have adequate information to have an effective confrontation. Now, some Christians will use such a retreat method as a cop-out and say, "I'm just praying about the situation." Years later, they are still fuming and praying about it. Don't retreat longer than is necessary.

EXPRESSING YOUR NEEDS

The following exercise will help you to stop retreating when you should be expressing your needs. It will be helpful to anyone who has ever acted as an Abdicator—which is probably pretty much everyone, at some point—to see areas in his or her life where needs have not been addressed.

The "I" Statement

In developing our spiritual maturity, we must perfect the ability to express our needs, preferences, or desires to another in a non-accusatory, non-blaming, and non-judgmental manner. We do this through the use of an "I" statement. The model of the "I" statement is as follows:

I feel _____
(the emotion evoked by the offensive or hurtful behavior; for example, angry, annoyed, unappreciated, frustrated, disrespected, etc.)

when you _____.
(specific, non-blaming, non-accusatory, or non-judgmental description of the behavior)

I would prefer that you _____.
(exactly what you'd like to see happen)

Let's try a few situations to get into practice.

Friend to Friend

The Mature Way

"I feel annoyed when you criticize the message on my answering machine. I would appreciate it if you would simply leave your message and refrain from judging the content or length of my recording."

The Wrong Way

"Why are you always so critical? Why can't you just leave a message on the answering machine like everyone else!"

The Abdicator

Wife to Husband

The Mature Way

"I really desire to feel pampered by you. When you ignore my dirty car, I don't feel pampered. I would really appreciate it if you would take my car to the car wash sometimes."

The Wrong Way

"Do you ever think about anyone except yourself? Look at my car. It is filthy while your car sits there sparkling clean! What kind of a husband treats his wife like that?"

Relative to Relative

The Mature Way

"I feel really frustrated when you forget to tell me about family events in a timely manner. Last-minute notices do not allow me the time to adjust my schedule. I would appreciate as much advance notice as possible so that I may plan to attend."

The Wrong Way

"Why do you people do everything at the last minute? Haven't you ever heard of the word P-L-A-N? I have a life. I can't just change my schedule at a moment's notice to attend these impromptu gatherings!"

Spouse to Spouse

The Mature Way

"I felt really embarrassed when you corrected my grammar in front of those people tonight. Next time, I would appreciate it if you would correct me in private."

The Wrong Way

"Why are you so picky? You didn't have to try to make me look bad in front of those people. Their grammar isn't so perfect either. Besides, they understood what I was talking about, didn't they?"

* * * * *

The Mature Way

"I feel very insignificant when I come home from work and you do not get up from the computer to greet me. I would be really pleased if you'd stop working long enough to interact with me for a few minutes."

The Wrong Way

"I guess that work is more important than I am. Why, you can't even break away from it long enough to say hello! I'm going to start acting the same way so that you can see how it feels to be ignored!"

Subordinate to Boss

The Mature Way

"I feel unappreciated when you individually praise or acknowledge everyone else's contribution to the project and say nothing about my efforts. Next time I'd like to know if my input is valued."

The Wrong Way

"I wish somebody would recognize my contribution to these projects. Why, everybody draws from my experience. And what do I get? Nothing!"

The Abdicator

Summary

Notice that in each "Wrong Way" instance, the confronting party was either judging, blaming, or accusing the other of negative behavior, rather than calmly stating what behavior he or she would prefer. Such approaches will most certainly prove to be counterproductive when working at overcoming Abdicator attitudes.

We need to meditate upon and embrace Isaiah 50:4 so that we can begin to exercise *"the tongue of the learned"* and to *"know how to speak a word in season."* We will then no longer abdicate our responsibility to express our needs.

Chapter Six

The Collaborator

Now we've come to the last confrontation style. The Collaborator deals with conflict much differently than the other styles I have discussed. One who collaborates when dealing with conflict does so by cooperating, joining forces, uniting, pulling together, participating, and co-laboring.

"LET'S FIND A WAY"

Before we discuss the Collaborator, let's briefly discuss the person who confronts ineffectively, who attempts to focus on the problem through indirect means. His actions range from throwing hints, making subtle jokes or sarcastic remarks, or just talking to the air when the offender is within earshot. He hopes that the offender will get the message. Even if the offender does get the message, he won't appreciate the indirect approach.

To collaborate means to work or act together toward a common end or purpose. Because the Collaborator cares about the relationship, the other person's well-being, or the organizational goals, he feels compelled to confront. He doesn't circle the airport on problematic issues; he lands the plane. He is emotionally balanced enough not to fear the reactions to a confrontation.

Collaborators are not deterred by rank, education, possessions, or policies. They are emotionally secure. Christians should be the most secure and confident people in any situation. *"If God is for us, who can be against us?"* (Rom. 8:31). *"The LORD is my light and my salvation; whom shall I fear?"* (Ps. 27:1). People who confront directly know what they desire and are not afraid to pursue it.

THE DAUGHTERS OF ZELOPHEHAD: ASKING FOR WHAT YOU WANT

The five daughters of Zelophehad set a shining example of an effective confrontation. The Israelites were about to possess the Promised Land. The daughters of Zelophehad were well aware of the guidelines that had been established for allocating the land among various families. However, they felt that these laws were unfair since it denied them their rights to inherit property owned by their deceased father. They decided to confront Moses and the elders.

Then came the daughters of Zelophehad the son of Hepher, the son of Gilead, the son of Machir, the son of Manasseh, from the families of Manasseh the son of

Joseph; and these were the names of his daughters: Mahlah, Noah, Hoglah, Milcah, and Tirzah. And they stood before Moses, before Eleazar the priest, and before the leaders and all the congregation, by the doorway of the tabernacle of meeting, saying: "Our father died in the wilderness; but he was not in the company of those who gathered together against the LORD, in company with Korah, but he died in his own sin; and he had no sons. Why should the name of our father be removed from among his family because he had no son? Give us a possession among our father's brothers." So Moses brought their case before the LORD. And the LORD spoke to Moses, saying: "The daughters of Zelophehad speak what is right; you shall surely give them a possession of inheritance among their father's brothers, and cause the inheritance of their father to pass to them."

(Num. 27:1–7)

These were some brave women who took matters into their own hands. They had no men in their lives to speak on their behalf—no father, no husbands, no brothers, and no sons. Yes, they had uncles, but it was unlikely that they would be supporting the women in their request since they were asking for land that would, under the current plan, default to the uncles (v. 4).

There are several lessons that we can learn from their actions.

Lesson One:

They went directly to the people who could change the situation. Already part of a multitude prone to grumbling, they could have easily gone throughout the camp mumbling and complaining about the inequities of their situation. (I've often wondered if they were the only ones in this predicament.) Their going before Moses and the entire congregation was tantamount to a congressional hearing, and not one that they were summoned to, but one that they called! It must have taken tremendous courage to be such trailblazers.

Lesson Two:

They were very clear as to what they wanted. Many times in a conflict, we don't articulate what we really want to happen or to stop happening. Sometimes we don't quite know what we want and therefore confront prematurely. But this is not case with the Zelophehad women. They clearly wanted the same type of allocation that their uncles had gotten.

Notice that they did not have to burn their bras, so to speak, or abandon their femininity. Furthermore, there is no evidence of any hostility on their part; they simply asked for what they wanted. Confrontation does not have to be hostile!

Lesson Three:

They were not deterred by set policies or tradition. Sure, God had given Moses the mandate to distribute the land only to those males who had been numbered (Num. 26), and who would thus help to conquer the Promised Land; the women weren't numbered. The daughters of Zelophehad were asking God to change His plan! Even God can be flexible to fulfill His divine destiny.

How many times have you walked away disappointed in various situations upon hearing that something you've just requested is against company policy? Such a statement is always my cue to take my need to the next level of management. Don't be afraid to ask to be the exception to the policy. *"Ye have not, because ye ask not"* (James 4:2 KJV). I rarely take "no" for an answer. Perseverance is a good character trait worth developing. It also does wonders for your self-esteem and confidence. And besides, we will never receive some benefits unless we ask for them.

Lesson Four:

They made their request on a timely basis. We could minimize and even avoid the impact of potential conflicts if we would speak up while there's still time to take action. *"A prudent man foreseeth the evil, and hideth* [i.e., protects] *himself; but the simple pass on, and are punished"* (Prov. 27:12 KJV). The Zelophehad Five spoke up while they were still in the wilderness; the land had not even been conquered. There's nothing like planning. We can't afford to sit around and assume that everyone is thinking about our welfare. After the raises are announced is not the time to petition your boss for your increase!

Our courage to confront can often improve the quality of life, not only for ourselves, but for others as well. Not only were the daughters granted an inheritance in the Promised Land, but God also changed the rules for future generations.

> *And thou shalt speak unto the children of Israel, saying, If a man die, and have no son, then ye shall cause his inheritance to pass unto his daughter. And if he have no daughter, then ye shall give his inheritance unto his brethren. And if he have no brethren, then ye shall give his inheritance unto his father's brethren. And if his father have no brethren, then ye shall give his inheritance unto his kinsman that is next to him of his family, and he shall possess it: and it shall be unto the children of Israel a statute of judgment, as the LORD commanded Moses.* *(Num. 27:8–11 KJV)*

Yes, God is for women's rights. It's possible that women wouldn't own land today had it not been for these courageous daughters. By the way, aren't you glad that Moses was not a Dictator? He could have easily said, "Sorry, the policy is set. You women go back home and don't make any more trouble." Rather, he took the case to God. Thank you, Moses, for being a Collaborator.

Lesson Five:

The women maintained a win-win attitude. Just when they were ready to relax after their major victory of getting their request granted, they found that the conflict was not yet over. The uncles later determined that they had a problem with the revised plan. If the daughters of Zelophehad were to marry outside of the tribe, their land would increase the holdings of their husbands' tribes. They sought to avoid such dilution. Now it was back to the negotiating table.

> *Then at the Lord's command Moses gave this order to the Israelites: "What the tribe of the descendants of Joseph is saying is right. This is what the LORD commands for Zelophehad's daughters: They may marry anyone they please as long as they marry within the tribal clan of their father. No inheritance in Israel is to pass from tribe to tribe, for every Israelite shall keep the tribal land inherited from his forefathers. Every daughter who inherits land in any Israelite tribe must marry someone in her father's tribal clan, so that every Israelite will possess the inheritance of his fathers. No inheritance may pass from tribe to tribe, for each Israelite tribe is to keep the land it inherits." So Zelophehad's daughters did as the LORD commanded Moses. Zelophehad's daughters—Mahlah, Tirzah, Hoglah, Milcah and Noah—married their cousins on their father's side.* (Num. 36:5–11 NIV)

Verse ten shows their willingness to be flexible. They could have said, "Wait, a deal is a deal. This looks like a breach of contract. Call the attorneys." A lawsuit certainly would have ensued had this situation occurred in today's litigious society.

In order to successfully resolve conflict where both sides have legitimate arguments, it is critical that all parties maintain win-win attitudes. Such was the case here. The daughters would still get their inheritance, and the uncles would not have to worry about dilution of the tribal inheritance.

DANIEL VERSUS MELZAR: TO EAT OR NOT TO EAT KOSHER

When King Nebuchadnezzar besieged Jerusalem, he took the inhabitants captive. Included in this group were several young men of royal descent. They were handsome and bright, and the king desired to train them for palace service. They were entered into a three-year special training program that included a prescribed diet. Daniel had a problem with the idea of eating the type of food to be provided. So he looked for an alternate plan.

But Daniel purposed in his heart that he would not defile himself with the portion of the king's delicacies, nor with the wine which he drank; therefore he requested of the chief of the eunuchs that he might not defile himself. Now God had brought Daniel into the favor and goodwill of the chief of the eunuchs. And the chief of the eunuchs said to Daniel, "I fear my lord the king, who has appointed your food and drink. For why should he see your faces looking worse than the young men who are your age? Then you would endanger my head before the king." So Daniel said to the steward [Melzar] whom the chief of the eunuchs had set over Daniel, Hananiah, Mishael, and Azariah, "Please test your servants for ten days, and let them give us vegetables to eat and water to drink. Then let our appearance be examined before you, and the appearance of the young men who eat the portion of the king's delicacies; and as you see fit, so deal with your servants." So he consented with them in this matter, and tested them ten days. And at the end of ten days their features appeared better and fatter in flesh than all the young men who ate the portion of the king's delicacies. Thus the steward took away their portion of delicacies and the wine that they were to drink, and gave them vegetables. (Dan. 1:8–16)

Daniel is one of the most politically savvy and spiritually mature characters in the Bible. Notice the wisdom and the respect with which he approached Melzar regarding his desire to abstain from the not-so-kosher meal plan. He had already decided that he was definitely not going to partake, yet he *"requested"* (v. 8) permission to follow a vegetarian diet instead. His requesting assured Melzar that Daniel respected his authority; he was not being a rebellious subject. Many Christians have been disdained and even disadvantaged in the workplace, not for their holy stand, but for how they communicated it to those in charge: "I don't attend parties where heathens are drinking!" Where is the wisdom in this?

Daniel demonstrated additional wisdom in offering a win-win alternative to the king's diet plan. Yet, as we look at this story, it's important to remember that it wasn't Daniel's astuteness that caused Melzar to give his proposal a chance, but God's *"favor"* (v. 9). While we may be adamant about seeking the highest level of competence and honing our communication and other necessary skills to do a job well, in the final analysis it is God who gives us favor with man. We must never lose sight of this reality.

We must remember to ask God for such favor. He has often given me favor with people with whom I least expected to have it and with whom I have even had an adversarial relationship. In fact, when I was promoted to a vice president at a major entertainment conglomerate, the man who made the nomination to the board of directors had caused me much grief in the past. Who can figure God out? *"The king's heart is in the hand of the LORD, as the rivers of water: he turneth it whithersoever he will"* (Prov. 21:1 KJV).

Part III

Steps to an Effective Confrontation

Chapter Seven

Preparing for the Encounter

The ability to confront effectively is learned behavior. The more we practice it, the better we become at it. Just as a wonderful physique is developed by frequent trips to the gym and using correct muscle building techniques, good confrontation skills must be constantly exercised for them to become effective. In this chapter and the ones that follow in this section, I will discuss how you can best prepare for confrontation and the steps that you can practice in your confrontations.

GO WITH THE RIGHT PURPOSE

The first step in preparing for a confrontation is to establish the right purpose for the proposed meeting. The focus should be on achieving a better relationship or getting someone to stop doing something that is negatively impacting you, others, or himself. The purpose should not be to tell someone off or to get something off your chest.

Confront yourself first. Be honest about why you're confronting. Is your motive pure? It is important to first pray about the situation. Get God's mind and insight on the matter. Isaiah 55:11 tells us, *"So is my word that goes out from my mouth: it will not return to me empty, but will accomplish what I desire and achieve the purpose for which I sent it"* (NIV).

So, ask yourself, "When this confrontation is over, what would I like to see changed?" Remember that an effective confrontation should get the desired effect. Unity or agreement should be the ultimate goal. That's where the blessing is given.

SELECT THE RIGHT TIME AND PLACE

There is a time for everything. There is a time to confront and a time not to confront. This doesn't mean that you abandon the idea of a confrontation, but that you wait until the appropriate time. In a work situation, you'll not want to confront right before lunch or at closing time or any other time when the person is preoccupied with another matter. Confronting when the person is most receptive to a serious discussion takes some forethought and planning.

Wife, when your husband first comes home from work, give him space to settle down first before you bombard him with the problems of the day. Husband, don't wait until you arrive at the event to tell your wife that you do not like the outfit that she is wearing. Tell her when she can do something about it!

If at all possible, try to confront a person when he is alone. Confronting someone in the presence of another can only cause him to become defensive to save face. Telephone confrontations are not the most desirable. After all, confrontation is coming together face-to-face. With call waiting features and so forth, incoming calls can interrupt the flow of conversation. Direct personal contact allows the parties to observe each other's facial expressions and to engage in more effective listening. If you have something really heavy to tell someone, it is not a good idea to have the confrontation at his house or yours. You'll want to select a neutral location that is conducive to good conversation. It will be easier for the confronted to leave the scene if he becomes belligerent. There is always the possibility that this could happen. Sometimes you have to lose people first to win them later. According to Proverbs 28:23, *"he who rebukes a man will find more favor afterward than he who flatters with the tongue."* We must be willing to take the risk.

Writing a letter may be better than a face-to-face confrontation if the person to be confronted has a stronger personality than you and you feel certain that you will not be able to get a word in edgewise. I only encourage letter writing as the last resort.

Preparing for confrontation is almost as important as the confrontation encounter itself. Confronting someone spontaneously or without any preparation, even in a situation where confrontation is most needed, might have disastrous results. Preparation allows you to look at the situation more clearly, and not in the midst of an emotional moment, and this will most likely lead to a more effective encounter. Keep in mind also that prayer is always the best preparation.

Chapter Eight

Owning the Problem

The next step involved in an effective confrontation is owning the problem. In any confrontation, it is important that we speak on our own behalf. We must own the problem. We must explain how a person's behavior has impacted us directly or how we are personally perceiving a problem. This is a straightforward approach that shows our strength. Not owning the problem when we do in fact have an issue with the person's behavior is a cowardly act.

In the work environment, it is especially critical to describe the impact that the problem is having on you as well as the others. I have seen people attempt to confront by not owning the issue personally. They'll say, "Some people think you..." rather than "I've noticed that you...."

I once had to confront a young man whose terrible grammar was hindering his career. I had overheard some management executives say so. Before I approached him, I purchased a grammar book. When I met with him, he immediately became defensive and asserted that management was unfair and that his grammar was fine. Because I had a genuine interest in his success, I then told him that I agreed that his grammar needed improvement. I owned the problem. I gave him the book and encouraged him to use it. He later thanked me for how I had handled the matter. Confrontations are never easy but can yield life-changing results.

KING ACHISH VERSUS DAVID: "STOP, YOU'RE HURTING THE ORGANIZATION!"

The Philistines gathered all their forces at Aphek, and Israel camped by the spring in Jezreel. As the Philistine rulers marched with their units of hundreds and thousands, David and his men were marching at the rear with Achish. The commanders of the Philistines asked, "What about these Hebrews?" Achish replied, "Is this not David, who was an officer of Saul king of Israel? He has already been with me for over a year, and from the day he left Saul until now, I have found no fault in him." But the Philistine commanders were angry with him and said, "Send the man back, that he may return to the place you assigned him. He must not go with us into battle, or he will turn against us during the fighting. How better could he regain his master's favor than by taking the heads of our own men? Isn't this the David they sang about in their dances: 'Saul has slain his thousands, and David his tens of thousands'?" So Achish called David and said to him, "As surely as the LORD lives, you have been reliable, and I would be pleased to have you serve with me in the army. From the day you came to me until now, I have found no fault in you, but the rulers don't approve of you. Turn back and go in peace; do nothing to displease the Philistine rulers." "But what have I done?" asked David. "What have you found against your servant from the day I came to you until now? Why can't I go and fight against the enemies of my lord the king?" Achish answered, "I know that you have been as pleasing in my eyes as an angel of God; nevertheless, the Philistine commanders have said, 'He must not go up with us into battle.' Now get up early, along with your master's servants who have come with you, and leave in the morning as soon as it is light." So David and his men got up early in the morning to go back to the land of the Philistines, and the Philistines went up to Jezreel. (1 Sam. 29:1–11 NIV)

David, in fleeing the wrath of Saul, king of Israel, had sought political asylum with Israel's enemy, the Philistines. Although David had slain their giant, God had given him favor with the Philistine leader, King Achish. During his time in Philistia, David had convinced the king that he had conducted several successful raids against the Israelites, even though he had not.

In this Scripture passage, the Israelite army and the Philistine army were preparing for battle again. David foolishly asked King Achish for permission to fight in the battle against his own people. Having no reason to question David's loyalty, the king obliged him.

When David and his men showed up for battle, the Philistine commanders immediately suspected their motives. They were appalled that King Achish could be so gullible. Didn't he realize that David could use this as an opportunity to get back into King Saul's good grace by turning on the Philistines in the battle?

They insisted that King Achish send David and his men back to their assigned place away from the battle. Can't you see the hand of God rescuing David from his precarious position? Imagine the future king of Israel with the blood of his own people on his hands!

King Achish was in a predicament. He had to confront David, whom he trusted, on behalf of his commanders who wanted him dismissed. He could not speak on his own behalf, for he didn't share their mistrust. However, the cohesiveness of the entire army hung in the balance. The king knew that he had to do what was best for the organization.

As a former corporate manager, I've found myself in a similar plight on a few occasions. I have had subordinates whom I personally liked and who interacted with me quite favorably. However, they wreaked havoc on the rest of the staff. Eventually, I was compelled to act in the best interest of the organization. When the buck stops with us, we must always do what is best for the whole. One bad apple really can spoil the whole bunch.

I can identify with the king's anguish as he tried to let David down easy. *"I have found no fault in you, but the rulers don't approve of you"* (v. 6). David then attempted to convince the king to let him stay.

The key conflict management lessons having to do with owning the problem, which can be learned from this story, are the following.

Lesson One:

Once we know that we have made the right decision, we must not allow ourselves to be persuaded otherwise, not by emotions, not by personalities, and not by our own personal desires. King Achish answered each of David's rebuttals in the same manner. He simply stated that David's presence would have had a detrimental effect on the rest of the army. Therefore, he had to leave the battlefield. The king used the broken record approach. This can be very effective when one must stand his ground.

Lesson Two:

Conflict must be confronted on a timely basis to minimize further negative impact. Although King Achish loved David, he addressed the problem of his presence before any real damage could be done to the army.

Many times we tolerate a situation too long before we address it. Often, irreparable damage is done. I know of a church where the pastor allowed one strong-willed member to systematically alienate every other key worker until almost all programs of the church virtually ceased. The last that I heard about this pastor was that he was trying desperately to recruit the former members. They had all gone to greener, more worker-friendly pastures.

Chapter Nine

Speaking with the Tongue
of the Learned

Words are our tools of communication. Words never die. They live on and on in the heart of the hearer. To maintain harmonious relationships in every facet of our lives, we must learn to use words effectively. In His infinite wisdom, God has already equipped us to speak words that get the desired results: *"The Lord GOD hath given me the tongue of the learned, that I should know how to speak a word in season to him that is weary"* (Isa. 50:4 KJV). In this chapter, I will address the next step involved in confronting effectively, which is speaking in this way, *"with the tongue of the learned."*

BE SPECIFIC

In confronting others, it is important to cite specific facts and incidents to describe exactly what we've observed or experienced. Beating around the bush or circling the airport just doesn't work. Such evasiveness may cause the point to be missed or may lead to a misunderstanding of what we are really trying to say. It is not sufficient to tell me just to use more wisdom around another woman's husband. You need to say, "Deborah, I'm sure you meant no harm, but it was inappropriate for you to straighten Jim's tie as you did on Sunday."

If your boss has excluded you from a meeting that involved your department, why not say, "Mary, my being excluded from that meeting on Wednesday has caused some real problems. I'd like to discuss them with you." Then, go on to list specific consequences, such as inability to meet a deadline, and so forth. You must focus on the person's actions and not his character. Stay calm; you're working toward a solution. There is no need to get emotional.

Talking in general terms is simply not effective. It also makes it easy for someone to deny any wrongdoing or to misinterpret the message.

Jenny's Story

Jenny, the pastor's wife, found herself in a real dilemma. Susan, one of their parishioners who was an attractive female, had developed a real burden for the first family—more specifically, for Bob, the pastor. She would bring him special gifts that often could not be shared by the family. She would call him at home occasionally for casual encouragement chats. Jenny grew increasingly uncomfortable with Susan's familiarity with her husband but held her peace. She feared that Bob would get upset and accuse her of being jealous. "Perhaps," Jenny mused, "my insecurity is working overtime since I've gained a considerable amount of weight." She prayed with her prayer partner, who urged her to discuss the issue with Bob. Of course, Bob seemed totally oblivious to Susan's little improprieties.

One day Jenny was called out of town to assist an ailing relative. Upon returning home several days later, she walked into her kitchen only to find Susan preparing dinner for the family! Jenny was livid, but she said nothing to Susan. She politely thanked her for her efforts to help them out. Later that night, she confronted Bob about the entire situation. He was shocked that Jenny had even entertained any negative thoughts about Susan's motives. He was certain that she was only trying to help. Needless to say, he dismissed Jenny's suggestion that he have a talk with her. Consequently, the unwise behavior continued.

Finally, Jenny decided that the situation was taking too heavy a toll on her emotions and her spiritual life. She was beginning to resent Bob for minimizing her concern and felt deep anger toward Susan for her insensitivity. Jenny had kept quiet for the sake of peace but was far from experiencing inner peace. She knew what she had to do.

She phoned Susan at her office and asked if they could meet. When they met, the gist of the conversation was as follows:

Jenny: "Thank you, Susan, for taking time out of your lunch hour to see me."

Susan: "Oh, it's no problem. I'm always available to you and Pastor Bob."

Jenny: "I know, I know. In fact, that's what I want to talk to you about. I need you to help me protect my husband's reputation. I'm sure that you're not aware of it, but

I've noticed several actions on your part that would cause me and others to look askance at Bob. For instance, [several incidences noted]. In light of these, I felt that I should speak to you about them."

Susan: "I am shocked [tears, tears] that you feel this way! I was just trying to be of service to you both. I won't even speak to him again if that makes you happy. I'm sorry that I ever extended myself at all [more tears]."

Jenny: "I didn't come down here to upset you. I just wanted you to know the impact that your behavior was having on me personally and the potential impact on Bob's ministry. I hope that we can continue to maintain a relationship—one that honors God and that will be mutually rewarding. Do you mind if we pray together now?"

The story above is true; the names have been changed to protect the identities of the parties. I applaud Jenny for her initiative; however, the situation should have been handled by Bob. Even though he is a pastor and a spiritual leader, his style is to avoid conflict. He is a real Abdicator. Notice that Jenny owned the issue. She didn't say, "Some of the members are talking." She didn't accuse. She simply presented the facts.

THE IMPORTANCE OF CRITICISM

No one enjoys receiving or giving criticism. Like the words *diet* and *confrontation,* the word *criticism* has gotten a bad rap and a generally accepted negative definition because of its association with negative situations. In fact, the true definition of criticism is "the act of making a judgment based on analysis and evaluation." To learn to receive and to give criticism like a pro, you must change your mind-set about the purpose of criticism.

Constructive Criticism

I've learned that good, constructive criticism can provide me with information I can use to grow. Information is power. If I have information on how I am perceived or how my behavior is affecting those around me, I can more effectively achieve my goals in my personal and business dealings.

The word *constructive* denotes that which builds. Negative comments about a person's character or judgment do not build, but rather tear down. Never put another person down. When you make fun, belittle, or ridicule somebody, especially in front of others, you have just created a real enemy. Always be careful to preserve the dignity of another person, Christian or non-Christian. Do unto others as you would have them do unto you.

Once I was at a client's office and witnessed an awful confrontation between two Christians of the opposite sex. She attacked his manhood; he attacked her womanhood. The rest of the staff was stunned and dismayed by their outburst. As a Christian I was quite embarrassed. I know God was ashamed; Satan had gotten a victory.

We must always remember that in any response to conflict, the focus should be on the person's behavior, not his *personhood,* that is, his personality, judgment, or character. The more spiritually mature we are, the more able we are to disconnect a person from his behavior. God has set the example. He hates sin, but loves the sinner. When Jesus confronted the woman caught in adultery, He told her that He did not condemn her. But He also admonished her to *"go and sin no more"* (John 8:11). He disconnected her sin from her personhood.

We are quick to make an accusation, even before we get all of the facts. Learn to practice objectivity. The ability to see both sides of the issue can make you a great peace-maker. Let's look at another biblical example.

Jethro versus Moses: "What You Are Doing Is Not Good"

The next day Moses took his seat to serve as judge for the people, and they stood around him from morning till eve-ning. When his father-in-law saw all that Moses was do-ing for the people, he said, "What is this you are doing for the people? Why do you alone sit as judge, while all these people stand around you from morning till evening?" Moses answered him, "Because the people come to me to seek God's will. Whenever they have a dispute, it is brought to me, and I decide between the parties and in-form them of God's decrees and laws." Moses' father-in-law replied, "What you are doing is not good. You and these people who come to you will only wear yourselves out. The work is too heavy for you; you cannot handle it alone. Listen now to me and I will give you some advice, and may God be with you. You must be the people's repre-sentative before God and bring their disputes to him. Teach them the decrees and laws, and show them the way to live and the duties they are to perform. But select capa-ble men from all the people—men who fear God, trustwor-thy men who hate dishonest gain—and appoint them as officials over thousands, hundreds, fifties and tens. Have them serve as judges for the people at all times, but have them bring every difficult case to you; the simple cases they can decide themselves. That will make your load lighter, because they will share it with you. If you do this and God so commands, you will be able to stand the strain, and all these people will go home satisfied." Moses listened to his father-in-law and did everything he said.
(Exod. 18:13–24 NIV)

Here we have a glimpse of the administrative side of life in the wilderness after the Israelites' great deliverance from Egypt. We see Moses in his new roles as interpreter of

God's laws and conflict consultant, among other things. Moses was obviously a man of great patience and discipline to be able to sit all day and listen to the problems and issues of the multitude. Thank God for the intervention of Jethro, Moses' father-in-law. We can learn the following lessons from this instance where Jethro confronted Moses.

Lesson One:

We can criticize with ease when we have earned the right to do so. Jethro was not just Moses' father-in-law, he was his former employer (Exod. 3:1), who willingly released Moses to return to Egypt to free the Israelites (Exod. 4:18). He had provided for Moses' family until the Israelites were safely in the wilderness; then he had reunited them with Moses (Exod. 18:5). He had been sincerely glad for all of God's goodness to Israel (v. 9); he was not envious that Moses had been exalted to such an honorable position as head of all Israel. He was not looking for ways to be critical. He cared about Moses and his welfare.

Lesson Two:

Criticism is more effective when coupled with a recommendation. To tell someone that "what you are doing is not good" can be very frustrating to the person if he is doing all that he knows to do. Jethro gave Moses a very concrete and workable suggestion. He also gave it in the right spirit: not as a mandate, but as an option for Moses to present to God. Further, he explained how the recommendation would personally benefit Moses as well as the multitude. This was no attempt to manipulate; this was pure love.

Lesson Three:

We must never become too big to be teachable. Moses readily accepted Jethro's advice despite the fact that

Jethro didn't have the face-to-face relationship with God that he enjoyed. Pride did not rule in Moses' life; he was the meekest man on the face of the earth (Num. 12:3).

Humbly Receiving Criticism

For some people, constructive criticism can be harder to receive because it forces them to acknowledge their fallibility. When we have established a reputation as a person of excellence in our endeavors, and as one to whom most people look as the source of knowledge and wisdom or as a role model in general, it can be very painful to face the fact that we may occasionally be wrong. We believe our own publicity; we buy into the image that others have of us. We enjoy that position on top of the pedestal. One of our greatest fears is the fear of falling off of it. In fact, trying to live up to that perfect image can be quite stressful and can cause us not to undertake endeavors that would prove to be rewarding and beneficial to others.

Until recently, I had a recurring dream of being at or near the top of a really high building or some other structure, and was always on the verge of falling. I'd often awaken with a sense of panic. After some deep introspection, I finally acknowledged that I had a fear of achieving great success; I feared that I would not be able to maintain it and would thus experience the humiliation of a great failure. I realized that I would have to find a way to abandon that need to be on top all the time.

Abandoning the Pedestal

In order to do this, I envision myself, in my mind's eye, calmly stepping down off the pedestal and joining the company of other excellence-seeking, fallible humans. The only one left on the pedestal is God; He's the standard.

Admitting Mistakes and Going Forward

Many excellence-oriented individuals whip themselves unmercifully for every single mistake. Rather than use mistakes as learning tools for future development, they reject their entire selves. They didn't merely make a mistake; they are a mistake. "How could I be so stupid?" they ask. Christians are particularly vulnerable to this attitude. Yet, if I were to ask a group of God-fearing Christians, "How many of you have sinned in the last month?" most would acknowledge that they had. Nevertheless, if I were to press further and ask, "How many consider yourselves sinners?" I would get no takers. After all, a sinner is one who practices sin as a lifestyle, not one who has committed his life to God, but sins occasionally!

Well, why not apply the same thinking when it comes to our mistakes? Why color your, or anyone else's, entire character with a single mistake? Acknowledge it, ask forgiveness for it, learn from it, face the consequences of it with courage, and get on with life's next challenge. This is the ultimate demonstration of spiritual and emotional maturity.

Another Model

King David provides a good model of this behavior. In 2 Samuel 12, Nathan the prophet confronted the king about the adultery he had committed with Bathsheba, the wife of Uriah, an officer in David's army. Bathsheba had conceived, and in his attempt to cover up his sin, David had her husband murdered in battle. Note the king's response to Nathan:

So David said to Nathan, "I have sinned against the LORD." And Nathan said to David, "The LORD also has put away your sin; you shall not die. However...the child also who is born to you shall surely die."

(2 Sam. 12:13–14)

King David did not excuse his behavior. He could have blamed Bathsheba for tempting him by bathing on the rooftop. He could have rationalized that he was overcome with the stress and pressures of being king. But no, he simply said, *"I have sinned."* The ability of anyone—the mighty or the lowly—to say, "I was wrong," is a mark of maturity that will endear one to family, coworkers, or others, much more than any attempt to make up for the wrongdoing. Furthermore, people who acknowledge their mistakes and forgive themselves are more apt to understand and forgive the mistakes of others. *"Forgive us our debts, as we forgive our debtors"* (Matt. 6:12).

King David did not allow his mistake or the child's death to immobilize him; he got on with the business of life. Notice his reaction when he was informed that the child had died:

And he said, While the child was yet alive, I fasted and wept: for I said, Who can tell whether GOD will be gracious to me, that the child may live? But now he is dead, wherefore should I fast? can I bring him back again? I shall go to him, but he shall not return to me. And David comforted Bathsheba his wife, and went in unto her, and lay with her: and she bare a son, and he called his name Solomon: and the LORD loved him.

(2 Sam. 12:22–24 KJV)

Solomon turned out to be the wisest man who ever lived. He was the product of a king who repented and went forward.

Destructive Criticism

Not all criticism is constructive; thus, not all criticism has to be accepted. Sometimes its goal is destructive; someone desires to tear you down, diminish your self-esteem, or manipulate you to accept his way of thinking. Always analyze the motive of a person who criticizes or critiques you. Ask yourself these thought-provoking questions:

- In the past, has this person demonstrated a genuine concern for my personal development?

- What does he have to gain personally if I adopt the behavior he is recommending to me? What do I have to gain?

- Is his attitude one of helpfulness, or am I feeling attacked or put down? (Don't confuse a person's frustration with an attack.)

- After he criticizes me, do I feel like a hopeless failure, or does he express faith in my ability to change?

- Is he committed to sticking with me through the change?

Your Challenge

So that you can better handle criticism, I suggest you go right now and stand before a mirror and practice saying, "I'm sorry, I was wrong." I challenge you to acknowledge your very next mistake to the person who is hurt by your words or actions. Resist the temptation to explain away or justify your actions when criticized. Experience a rise in your maturity gauge as well as a rise in the person's respect for you.

THE SANDWICH APPROACH

Conducting an effective confrontation is a lot like preparing a steak sandwich. A basic sandwich consists of bread, meat, and another piece of bread. The bread makes the eating of the sandwich more pleasurable. It is the first and last thing bitten. The steak is the meat of the matter, the real issue of the confrontation.

The bread is a positive statement that lays the foundation of the confrontation. It affirms the person's worth and your commitment to the relationship. The statement should be true and not empty flattery. For instance, before Beth tells her husband that she needs more personal attention from him, she might say, "John, I really appreciate what a good provider you are. I never have to worry about the bills being paid. Your sense of responsibility gives me great comfort." John can now receive information about what is making his wife unhappy. She continues, "I need more affection from you...." Remember not to say *but* or *however* after the bread; these words act as giant erasers of what was previously stated.

Sometimes the bread is more effective when put in the form of an open-ended question. Once we met one of Darnell's cousins, who was a young woman from Georgia in her early twenties, who was visiting our church. She was very exuberant and responsive to the pastor's message during the service. We went to dinner and had a great time. When she told us later that she did not go to church regularly, I jokingly said, "If we had known that you were a heathen, we wouldn't have treated you to dinner."

Now understand that Darnell and I regularly use this term lightheartedly in referring to wayward Christians, and the conversation had been lighthearted all day. She was offended by the remark, but I greatly admired how she dealt with it. About an hour later—okay, so she fumed a while—she asked me, "Deborah, what did you mean by the term *heathen*?" When I explained that we use it jokingly, she told me that she thought it was offensive. I apologized and made a note to include the incident in this book. Notice that she got clarification of my intentions before drawing a conclusion about the matter.

In using the sandwich approach, it's important to include the other piece of bread. This allows you to close the confrontation positively. Express your commitment to working toward a positive relationship. The person should leave knowing that you are rejecting his behavior and not him personally.

To reiterate, the opening bread and closing bread are absolute musts to make the meat more palatable. And besides, most people will focus longer on what they consider the negative, or the meat. So make the bread good.

Chapter Ten

Listening with Learned Ears

I have always relied on Isaiah 50:4 for faith to believe that God was giving me the wisdom to speak the right words, but recently, the Holy Spirit caused me to focus on the second part of the Scripture. The bold is my emphasis.

> *The Lord GOD has given me the tongue of the learned, that I should know how to speak a word in season to him who is weary. He awakens me morning by morning, **He awakens my ear to hear as the learned**.*

This Scripture reminds us that we are not only to speak with learned tongues, but we also need to listen with learned ears. Such listening is what is needed next in effective confrontation. By listening, we create a context or environment where people feel free to speak without fear of punishment, ridicule, or other repercussions. James 1:19 admonishes us to be *"swift to hear."*

Consider the following incident. My husband and I belong to a sixteen-thousand-member church. Needless to say, we have to do some skillful maneuvering on Sunday mornings to get a good seat near the front of the sanctuary. One particular Sunday, I ducked into the lady's room prior to the start of the next service. While refreshing my makeup, I got carried away in a conversation with another woman whom I'd never met before. I was enjoying our fellowship so much that I lost track of the time. When I came outside, my normally patient husband, who had been waiting, was quite perturbed. He reprimanded me for taking so long and reminded me that we had now forfeited our strategic position near the beginning of the line to get into church. Well, I immediately felt perturbed with him for being perturbed with me.

Before I could respond negatively, the Holy Spirit challenged me to *"hear as the learned"* (Isa. 50:4). I asked myself, "What is causing his frustration?" After all, he doesn't have a preference for where we sit in the sanctuary. I am the one who insists on sitting near the front. Then it hit me; I had frustrated his attempt to please me. When I asked him if this were so, he confirmed that my assessment of the situation was correct. He gets a great thrill out of pleasing me—and of course, I always express my pleasure with his efforts. I apologized for my insensitivity, and we had a great time in the service.

GOD VERSUS ADAM AND EVE: AN OPPORTUNITY TO EXPLAIN

We must remember to *"hear as the learned."* We must discipline ourselves to listen rather than to formulate a response to what is being said. Even if we think we already know all of the facts of an issue, it pays to ask for and listen to an explanation. Notice the approach God used when

He confronted Adam and Eve after they had eaten the forbidden fruit. He asked a series of questions and gave them space to explain their behavior before He pronounced judgment on them.

> *And they heard the voice of the LORD God walking in the garden in the cool of the day: and Adam and his wife hid themselves from the presence of the LORD God amongst the trees of the garden. And the LORD God called unto Adam, and said unto him,* **[Question 1]** *Where art thou? And he said, I heard thy voice in the garden, and I was afraid, because I was naked; and I hid myself. And he said,* **[Question 2]** *Who told thee that thou wast naked?* **[Question 3]** *Hast thou eaten of the tree, whereof I commanded thee that thou shouldest not eat? And the man said, The woman whom thou gavest to be with me, she gave me of the tree, and I did eat. And the LORD God said unto the woman,* **[Question 4]** *What is this that thou hast done? And the woman said, The serpent beguiled me, and I did eat.* (Gen. 3:8–13 KJV)

Of course, God already knew the answer to each of the questions He had asked. But even He, in His mercy and long-suffering, waited and heard their feeble excuses before banishing them from the Garden of Eden. Sincere questioning will often provide insight as to why a person resorted to his behavior. It also shows an earnest effort to understand his actions. Let's look at an example from the New Testament.

PETER VERSUS ANANIAS AND SAPPHIRA: "IS IT TRUE?"

> *But a certain man named Ananias, with Sapphira his wife, sold a possession. And he kept back part of the proceeds, his wife also being aware of it, and brought a certain part and laid it at the apostles' feet. But Peter said, "Ananias, why has Satan filled your heart to lie to*

*the Holy Spirit and keep back part of the price of the
land for yourself? While it remained, was it not your
own? And after it was sold, was it not in your own control? Why have you conceived this thing in your heart?
You have not lied to men but to God." Then Ananias,
hearing these words, fell down and breathed his last. So
great fear came upon all those who heard these things.
And the young men arose and wrapped him up, carried
him out, and buried him.* (Acts 5:1–6)

The biblical principle of asking before accusing was
also demonstrated in this story of Ananias and Sapphira.
Peter first questioned Ananias about his motive for lying
about the price he had received for the land that he had
sold. Of course, Ananias never had a chance to answer him
because he fell down and died. What had happened was
that after skimming a portion of the profits, he and his
wife, Sapphira, had subsequently donated the proceeds to
the church, pretending that they had donated all. However,
Peter did not assume that Sapphira was guilty also, and he
gave her the benefit of the doubt.

*Now it was about three hours later when his wife came
in, not knowing what had happened. And Peter answered her, "Tell me whether you sold the land for so
much?" She said, "Yes, for so much." Then Peter said to
her, "How is it that you have agreed together to test the
Spirit of the Lord? Look, the feet of those who have buried your husband are at the door, and they will carry
you out." Then immediately she fell down at his feet and
breathed her last. And the young men came in and
found her dead, and carrying her out, buried her by her
husband.* (vv. 7–10)

Dear saint of God, let's challenge ourselves to speak as
the learned and to hear as the learned. God has already
given us the tongue and the ears to do so.

ISRAEL VERSUS ISRAEL:
THE DANGER IN MAKING ASSUMPTIONS

The Promised Land had been conquered, and now it was time to settle into everyday life. Moses had previously allowed the Reubenites, the Gadites, and the half-tribe of Manasseh to inherit the land east of the Jordan River while the other nine and a half tribes settled on the west side. The two and a half tribes had diligently fought the enemies that inhabited Canaan. They had stood as one with their brothers. Now the battle was over; the land had been conquered.

Joshua demobilized the army and dismissed the easterners to return to their families. But not so fast, Joshua! Since the Jordan River would physically separate them from the western tribes and the center of worship, they feared that someday the descendants of the westerners would say to their descendants that they, the easterners, had no part in the worship of the God of Israel. Therefore, to prevent this potential problem, the easterners built a huge altar near the Jordan River to commemorate their involvement. Big mistake!

The westerners heard about the altar and prepared to go to war against their brothers. Rather than approaching the perceived offenders in a spirit of peace and understanding, the westerners launched into a litany of accusations.

When they went to Gilead—to Reuben, Gad and the half-tribe of Manasseh—they said to them: "The whole assembly of the LORD says: 'How could you break faith with the God of Israel like this? How could you turn away from the LORD and build yourselves an altar in rebellion against him now? Was not the sin of Peor enough for us? Up to this very day we have not cleansed ourselves from that sin, even though a plague fell on the community of the LORD! And are you now turning away from the LORD? If you rebel against the LORD today, tomorrow he will be angry with the whole community of Israel. If the land you possess is defiled, come over to the Lord's land, where the Lord's tabernacle stands, and share the land with us. But do not rebel against the LORD or against us by building an altar for yourselves, other than the altar of the LORD our God. When Achan son of Zerah acted unfaithfully regarding the devoted things, did not wrath come upon the whole community of Israel? He was not the only one who died for his sin.'"

(Josh. 22:15–20 NIV)

Isn't it frustrating when someone goes on and on with an accusation, and he's completely wrong? Before you're tempted to throw up your hands, discipline yourself to stand still until the barrage is over. Then respond in a calm manner.

Then Reuben, Gad and the half-tribe of Manasseh replied to the heads of the clans of Israel: "The Mighty One, God, the LORD! The Mighty One, God, the LORD! He knows! And let Israel know! If this has been in rebellion or disobedience to the LORD, do not spare us this day. If we have built our own altar to turn away from the LORD and to offer burnt offerings and grain offerings, or to sacrifice fellowship offerings on it, may the LORD himself call us to account. No! We did it for fear that some day your descendants might say to ours, 'What do you have to do with the LORD, the God of Israel? The LORD has made the Jordan a boundary between us and you—you Reubenites and Gadites! You have no share in the LORD.' So your descendants might cause ours to stop fearing the LORD. That is why we said, 'Let us get ready and build an altar—but not for burnt offerings or sacrifices.' On the contrary, it is to be a witness between us and you and the generations that follow, that we will worship the LORD at his sanctuary with our burnt offerings, sacrifices and fellowship offerings. Then in the future your descendants will not be able to say to ours, 'You have no share in the LORD.' And we said, 'If they ever say this to us, or to our descendants, we will answer: Look at the replica of the Lord's altar, which our fathers built, not for burnt offerings and sacrifices, but as a witness between us and you.' Far be it from us to rebel against the LORD and turn away from him today by building an altar for burnt offerings, grain offerings and sacrifices, other than the altar of the LORD our God that stands before his tabernacle." When Phinehas the priest and the leaders of the community—the heads of the clans of the Israelites—heard what Reuben, Gad and Manasseh had to say, they were pleased. (vv. 21–30 NIV)

The lessons that this example teaches us in averting, minimizing, or managing a conflict are the following.

Lesson One:

We should never make a decision or initiate an action that involves the affairs or the possessions of another without first consulting that person or group. We cannot assume that because our intentions are noble or innocent, or because the cause is worthy, everybody will be happy with our actions.

Once, when I still lived at home, my brother joined a Corvette car club. The only problem was that he was planning to use my Corvette! Imagine his disappointment when I told him that the car would not be available to him.

I have had other people, usually relatives, volunteer my time, talents, and even my home to others without any prior discussion. Obviously, this was before I learned to set boundaries in my life. The point is that, if we are to live in harmony with others, we must respect their boundaries. Remember, people do not judge our intentions, they judge our actions.

Lesson Two:

When we feel that our boundaries have been violated, we should not conclude that the violator had less than honorable motives. We should not prepare for war before we fully understand their intentions or objectives.

Notice that the westerners sent a delegation (vv. 13–14) to the easterners, not to understand why the altar was erected, but to *"go to war against them"* (v. 12). They assumed that the easterners were going to offer sacrifices on the altar. Such action would be in direct violation of the law, which required everyone to sacrifice at Shiloh. The westerners thought, "Why, these eastern rebels will bring down the wrath of God on all Israel."

It's amazing how many Christians are quick to believe the worst about their sisters and brothers—no matter what problems or experiences they've been through together. We can simply hear that someone made a negative comment about us, and we prepare to fight. What a sad commentary on our spiritual maturity.

Lesson Three:

We must always verify the truth of the matter before we make accusations. In verses sixteen through twenty, the westerners accused the easterners of wrongdoing and reminded them of times past when Israel had offended God. Verses twenty-one through twenty-nine record the easterners' defense. They give extensive detail on their thought process in initiating the altar. They simply wanted a memorial that would attest to their involvement west of the Jordan. Of course, if they had discussed the idea before their zealous act, the conflict would never have arisen.

Fortunately, this story has a happy ending. After the explanation was given, an understanding was achieved. To the credit of the western delegation, they heard the explanation. Even though they had come to fight, they took time to hear the other side. The explanation pleased them (v. 30).

Lesson Four:

When we are the perpetrators of questionable actions, we must be quick to provide an explanation. It is not enough that God knows. The easterners were appalled that their motives were misunderstood. *"The LORD God of gods, the LORD God of gods, he knoweth, and Israel he shall know"* (v. 22 KJV). Yes, our record may be written in heaven, but we live on earth among men! And men deserve an explanation and an apology when we offend them.

> *Therefore if thou bring thy gift to the altar, and there rememberest that thy brother hath ought against thee; leave there thy gift before the altar, and go thy way; first be reconciled to thy brother, and then come and offer thy gift.* (Matt. 5:23–24 KJV)

YOUR CHALLENGE

The next time you're attempting to resolve a conflict with someone, challenge your listening skills by waiting five complete seconds after the person finishes his statement before you respond. Put yourself in his shoes. Fully absorb all that he has said. Ask clarifying questions. Then calmly state your understanding of what the person has said. You will then find that your listening will be rewarded.

Chapter Eleven

Agreeing on Future Behavior

Agreeing on acceptable behavior after the confrontation is absolutely necessary for confronting effectively. It is an important key to maintaining harmony, even if the person who was confronted does not accept responsibility for his past actions. For example, he may insist that you had the wrong perception of his actions and that you are the one at fault. This could be the case. Nevertheless, it's important that you both agree on what you'll each do should a similar situation arise in the future. It may require mutual compromise. Someone may have to stop doing something; someone may have to start doing something. Whatever the decision, the approach should be win-win.

Even in the story of the daughters of Zelophehad, which was discussed in an earlier chapter, the daughters had the wisdom to compromise. They had received the land allocation for which they had petitioned, but they were willing to marry only men in their tribe so that their uncles' concerns would be addressed in a way that was mutually satisfying to everyone involved.

> "This is what the LORD commands for Zelophehad's daughters: They may marry anyone they please as long as they marry within the tribal clan of their father. No inheritance in Israel is to pass from tribe to tribe, for every Israelite shall keep the tribal land inherited from his forefathers. Every daughter who inherits land in any Israelite tribe must marry someone in her father's tribal clan, so that every Israelite will possess the inheritance of his fathers. No inheritance may pass from tribe to tribe, for each Israelite tribe is to keep the land it inherits." So Zelophehad's daughters did as the LORD commanded Moses. Zelophehad's daughters—Mahlah, Tirzah, Hoglah, Milcah and Noah—married their cousins on their father's side. They married within the clans of the descendants of Manasseh son of Joseph, and their inheritance remained in their father's clan and tribe.
>
> (Num. 36:6–12 NIV)

This was a win-win settlement. Agreement is particularly important when the behavior of one person or group will affect many others.

In a work environment, each person's role ultimately impacts the organizational goals; therefore, issues need to be resolved satisfactorily. And in addition to this, what will happen in the future needs to be discussed. If you've asked for a promotion or a raise, and the company has informed you that it won't be forthcoming, the supervisor and you, the employee, should agree on what you need to do to improve your chances of getting what you want. A specific time should be set to review the situation. This is what I mean by agreeing on future behavior. Then, you, the requester, may have to remind the supervisor that the time has come for the review. This is no time to be shy. This is being assertive—a necessary trait of a good communicator. Let's look at a story in which two men agreed on acceptable behavior after a confrontation.

PAUL AND BARNABAS: AGREEING TO DISAGREE

And some days after Paul said unto Barnabas, Let us go again and visit our brethren in every city where we have preached the word of the Lord, and see how they do. And Barnabas determined to take with them John, whose surname was Mark. But Paul thought not good to take him with them, who departed from them from Pamphylia, and went not with them to the work. And the contention was so sharp between them, that they departed asunder one from the other: and so Barnabas took Mark, and sailed unto Cyprus; and Paul chose Silas, and departed, being recommended by the brethren unto the grace of God. (Acts 15:36–40 KJV)

Here is the story of two spiritual giants who couldn't reconcile their differences. The disagreement between Paul and Barnabas was rooted in basic personality differences.

Paul, the decisive, no-nonsense, intelligent, focused apostle was unwilling to take John Mark, Barnabas's relative, on another missionary trip with them. On a prior trip, John Mark had become homesick and had left them high and dry. Paul must have reasoned that they were on a mission from God and had no time for flakes.

True to the meaning of his name, Barnabas was indeed the "son of encouragement." It was he who had brought Paul, soon after his conversion, to the skeptical disciples. He had vouched for Paul's credibility and had convinced them to accept him. He could not turn his back on anyone, especially a relative. After all, charity begins at home. Paul and Barnabas had conducted many great evangelistic revivals together. Theirs was no casual acquaintance. And now they found themselves at total odds with each other.

In reading this story, I am reminded of my stint in high school as a drum majorette. Coordination has never been my strong suit, but perseverance is. I was determined to be a part of the group that led the band out onto the football field for the halftime show. During my initial rehearsals, I had a difficult time keeping my line of musicians marching in a straight line. They were following me! When the line would veer to the right, Mr. Jones, our band leader, would yell at me like a drill sergeant, "Smith, straighten that line!" I'd do fine for a few minutes, and then I'd veer to the left. "Smith, straighten that line!"

Finally, in desperation, Mr. Jones gave me some advice that solved the problem. In my attempt to keep in step, I had been focusing on the majorettes on either side of me. He advised, "Keep your eyes on the drum major. Everyone who is in step with the drum major, will be in step with each other." What a powerful principle! I have applied this advice to my marriage and to numerous conflict situations, especially with Christians. Everybody who is in step with God will be in step with each other.

And so in this battle of wills, only one person could be right. The conflict management lessons to be learned are the following.

Lesson One:

No matter how spiritual a person is, everyone is subject to a blind spot when it comes to a relative. I have seen the most anointed ministers suffer long—too long—with a family member in a leadership or other critical position, to the detriment of the entire ministry. Rare is the leader who

has the objectivity to look beyond that blood bond and focus on the best for the organization. Equally rare is the
board of directors who has the courage to insist that a
change be made. Most boards will take an Accommodator
approach and let the minister have it his way. The king-
dom of God suffers for it.

Lesson Two:

We must actively work toward a mutually acceptable
resolution. When we fully grasp the truth that agreement
is the place of power, we will be more willing to yield so
that unity is achieved. Neither Paul nor Barnabas proposed an alternate solution, which would perhaps have
been another young man to assist them. Both dug in their
heels. Both took the "My Way" approach. Paul's stance
was: "I will not allow him to go." Barnabas's position was:
"I won't go without him."

Lesson Three:

We must be willing to seek outside help when we cannot resolve the problem. Jesus had given the procedures
for handling such conflict in Matthew 18.

> *Moreover if thy brother shall trespass against thee, go
> and tell him his fault between thee and him alone: if he
> shall hear thee, thou hast gained thy brother. But if he
> will not hear thee, then take with thee one or two more,
> that in the mouth of two or three witnesses every word
> may be established. And if he shall neglect to hear them,
> tell it unto the church: but if he neglect to hear the
> church, let him be unto thee as a heathen man and a
> publican.* (Matt. 18:15–17 KJV)

The next step was for Paul and Barnabas to seek the
help of other church members. But no such input was

sought. The church appeared to stand on the sidelines and let them battle it out. Even though a certain battle may be between only two individuals, those of us who see our brothers and sisters in conflict need to consider prayerfully our role as peacemakers. *"Blessed are the peacemakers: for they shall be called the children of God"* (Matt. 5:9 KJV). Peacemakers are people who actively seek to make peace. They initiate the unity efforts.

There is a risk in attempting to be a peacemaker. It is not a task for the fainthearted or the spiritually immature. Objectivity and confidentiality must be maintained as we attempt to get each party to come into agreement.

Lesson Four:

Sometimes the best resolution of a conflict is a separation, even if temporary. Now don't run out and divorce your spouse. I am simply saying that many times the parties are too emotionally attached to the issue and need space to regroup their thoughts. God is able to use separation for His glory. Because Paul and Barnabas separated, the Gospel was preached in even more cities. Should you decide that a temporary separation is the option, both parties should agree on how long it will be.

In some instances of friendships or other relationships, one party may have outgrown the relationship. Personally, I don't feel that it is necessary to acknowledge the end of a relationship. Some people may be too emotionally damaged by what they may perceive as rejection. Wisdom would dictate a phaseout instead. Not being available for most activities will usually convey the message. Of course, I'm a proponent of the direct approach in most situations, but we must be careful to consider the emotional and spiritual balance of situations in which we find ourselves in conflict.

Lesson Five:

When we determine that we have been wrong, we need to admit it. Often our erroneous assessments and assumptions cause conflict. In the case of Paul and Barnabas, Paul realized sometime later that John Mark really wasn't a flake. He asked Timothy to bring John Mark to him. *"Only Luke is with me. Take Mark, and bring him with thee: for he is profitable to me for the ministry"* (2 Tim. 4:11 KJV).

The ability to say, "I was wrong," is a real challenge for a Dictator type like Paul. But here he provides a shining example. Have you ever been wrong about someone and told him so later? I've had a few people confess to me that they had pegged me to be one way and later found out that they were wrong. I admired their courage to admit it. Of course, I questioned the wisdom of some of the confessions. It is not wise to tell someone, "I thought that you were stuck up because you drive a Mercedes, but I found out you're really down-to-earth!" And now, what is one to do with such revealing information?

Let's be careful to use wisdom in how much honest information to reveal. The Bible says that *"all things are lawful...but all things are not expedient"* (1 Cor. 6:12 KJV).

Lesson Six:

We must stay focused even when others don't take our sides. Acts 15:40 states that the Christian brothers gave Paul and Silas their blessings. There is no mention of their official support for Barnabas and Mark. Barnabas was not deterred by this. I've seen ministers criticize and even ostracize other ministers over issues of church hierarchy. To Paul and Barnabas's credit, we never read that either made negative statements about the other after the split. Both focused on their missions and brought glory to God.

Chapter Twelve

Forgiving and Forgetting

Volumes have been written on the importance of forgiveness. Yes, we know that if we don't forgive others, God won't forgive us. We know that unforgiveness can lead to physical and emotional problems. We know, we know, we know, but how do we get there? And we need to get there because it is the final step to an effective confrontation. It is the step that allows both parties of a confrontation to move on and away from the issue that led to the confrontation.

My experiences in forgiving have taught me a key lesson that will get any Spirit-filled Christian on the path. I was wrestling with a hurt recently and really wanted to get past it and to forgive the offending party, but I found that simply telling myself that I would forgive didn't stop the barrage of negative thoughts. I found myself continuing to rehearse the conversation that had led to the hurt. I really wanted to maintain a close relationship with the offender, but I couldn't get beyond the hurt. Then, like a flashlight in a dark tunnel, Philippians 2:13 exposed the heart of this dilemma: *"For it is God which worketh in you both **to will and to do** of his good pleasure"* (KJV, author's emphasis).

That's it! Forgiveness is not a natural response to a hurt or an offense; forgiveness requires supernatural intervention. My natural man wanted to see the person who had hurt me experience some pain too. But, my spiritual man wanted to do what would please God. I was trying too hard in my own strength to lick the problem. I just needed to let go and let God. I prayed, "Father, I thank You that Your Holy Spirit is already at work in me to give me the will to forgive. I delight in knowing that You don't leave a job half done. I receive Your power now to complete the work of forgiveness. I release all desire to avenge this wrong. You saw this situation before it happened, and in Your infinite wisdom, You allowed it to be so. I trust Your Word in Romans 8:28 that assures me that all things work together for my good because I love You and am called according to Your purpose. From this moment on, with the help of the Holy Spirit, I will not dwell on the situation but will declare Your Word instead. In Jesus' name, I pray. Amen."

I felt an immediate release from the bondage of unforgiveness. I once heard someone say that forgiveness is a decision to set a prisoner free and then a discovery that the prisoner was you. If you already have a desire to forgive someone who has offended you, get excited; the Holy Spirit has already done half the job.

RESIST RETALIATION

Recently, I went to our local post office to mail a package. As usual, for this particular post office, the line was quite long and moving very slowly. I joined the line behind a man who appeared to be in his early forties and who was obviously having a real problem with his sexuality. He wore heavy makeup and was clad in women's slacks and shoes. I mentally noted that he was shorter than I. Now, before I continue, I need to explain that my heart goes out to homosexuals. I believe that at the root of their deviation is a dysfunctional relationship, usually with the father; a childhood molestation; or some other work of Satan. Therefore, I am always pleasant toward them. When I am in their presence, I often pray under my breath for their deliverance.

Well, back to the story. Frustrated with the long line, the man started complaining loudly about the postal staff's inefficiency. He yelled that he wanted to see the manager. "This is ridiculous!" he shouted. "Every time I come here the service is terrible!" I started quietly agreeing with him, hoping that my doing so would calm him. Being the ever ready rescuer, I asked, "Are you in line just to buy a stamp? If so, I have one if you need it." "No," he replied hesitantly, "I need something else, too." After what seemed like an eternity, the manager appeared. The man tore into the manager by attacking his qualifications for the job. "Can't you control your staff?" he screamed. "You only have two people working the windows while everybody else is on break. You need to go back to school and learn how to manage!"

The manager did not respond to him directly. He simply began at the front of the line and attempted to find out which customers only needed stamps and which needed other services. He was clearly making an effort to expedite the process. As he got closer to us, Mr. Confused's remarks grew meaner. Not knowing what he might do next, I felt that I should do something to calm him. So I whispered to him, "Well, you've done a good job of getting his attention.

Let's just give him space now and see what he does." As I said this, I touched him lightly on his shoulder. Big mistake! He yelled, "Don't put your hands on me! Then he said, more calmly, "I know that you don't mean any harm, but don't put your hands on me."

Words cannot describe the humiliation and embarrassment I felt at his outburst. All eyes focused on me. Here I was trying to spare the manager public humiliation and look what I get. I resisted the urge to call him the politically incorrect name used to describe homosexuals. I also reminded myself that God wouldn't have been pleased if I had done so. "I must respond in a godly manner," I pleaded with my flesh. "After all, I teach others how to handle such situations." I remained silent as he continued to complain—albeit less loudly, praise God! Finally, he turned to me and asked, "Do you still have that stamp?"

Since I constantly study the Scriptures dealing with conflict, the Holy Spirit will usually bring one to my remembrance, if I'm listening. Today it was Proverbs 19:11: *"A man's wisdom gives him patience; it is to his glory to overlook an offense"* (NIV). I decided to respond just as the Scripture commanded, well sort of. I looked right over his head in stone silence! He wasn't getting my stamp after all.

The problem with retaliation is that it feels good to the flesh, but it grieves your spirit—and God's. I realized that in a subtle, passive-aggressive way, I had attempted to avenge the wrong that had been done to me. I had failed a spiritual test. Satan had gotten the victory. All that I could do was to repent.

Now, this incident may seem like a small thing, but we must remember that it's *"the little foxes that spoil the vines"* (Song 2:15). If we can begin to resist the temptation to retaliate in little things, we will develop retaliation-resistance muscles that will help us overlook larger offenses.

Let's look at an example from the Bible to illustrate the importance of forgiveness. This example also shows that retaliation is most definitely not needed for one to overcome a wrong done to him.

JEPHTHAH AND HIS NON-REPENTANT BROTHERS: NO FOOL TWICE

Now Jephthah the Gileadite was a mighty man of valour, and he was the son of an harlot: and Gilead begat Jephthah. And Gilead's wife bare him sons; and his wife's sons grew up, and they thrust out Jephthah, and said unto him, Thou shalt not inherit in our father's house; for thou art the son of a strange woman. Then Jephthah fled from his brethren, and dwelt in the land of Tob: and there were gathered vain men to Jephthah, and went out with him. And it came to pass in process of time, that the children of Ammon made war against Israel. And it was so, that when the children of Ammon made war against Israel, the elders of Gilead went to fetch Jephthah out of the land of Tob: and they said unto Jephthah, Come, and be our captain, that we may fight with the children of Ammon. And Jephthah said unto the elders of Gilead, Did not ye hate me, and expel me out of my father's house? and why are ye come unto me now when ye are in distress? And the elders of Gilead said unto Jephthah, Therefore we turn again to thee now, that thou mayest go with us, and fight against the children of Ammon, and be our head over all the inhabitants of Gilead. And Jephthah said unto the elders of Gilead, If ye bring me home again to fight against the children of Ammon, and the LORD deliver them before me, shall I be your head? And the elders of Gilead said unto Jephthah, The LORD be witness between us, if we do not so according to thy words. Then Jephthah went with the elders of Gilead, and the people made him head and captain over them: and Jephthah uttered all his words before the LORD *in Mizpeh. And Jephthah sent messengers unto the king of the children of Ammon, saying, What hast thou to do with me, that thou art come against me to fight in my land?*

(Judg. 11:1–12 KJV*)*

There are so many conflict and confrontation management lessons in this story that I'll try to contain myself and discuss only a few.

Lesson One:

Rejection is part of God's divine plan. Jephthah was rejected for a reason completely outside of his control; he was illegitimate. When he was cast out by his half brothers, he accepted it and went about his life. Many of us have experienced the emotional devastation of rejection. Some of us have been rejected because we are one or more of the following: white, black, too black, old, young, intelligent, dumb, pretty, ugly, privileged, poor, attractive, unattractive, sophisticated, or unsophisticated. This list is endless! The crux of the matter is that we are different. What has helped me to cope with such rejection is the assurance of divine destiny. Through it all, God has had a plan for my life. Every hurt, every rejection, and every disappointment has made me who I am today.

It was rejection that forced Jephthah to the land of Tob. Most likely, it was there that he learned and perfected the art of war. He became a mighty warrior. If he had been accepted by his brothers and stayed home with them, he would have been in the same helpless position as they were when the Ammonites came against the Gileadites. Notice that he never sought to do them harm for rejecting him.

Lesson Two:

We do not have to be a fool twice. Jephthah was not so emotionally dysfunctional and needy that he jumped at the chance to be in a relationship with his brothers again. Notice that when they asked him to come and be their captain, they never said that they were sorry for casting him out, or that they had had a change of heart and now wanted to embrace him. They simply needed a warrior to lead them in battle.

Not missing the motive, Jephthah responded by saying something like this: "Wait a minute. We can't just go forward as if nothing has happened. Our relationship has been damaged. Sounds like you just want to use me, since you're only coming to me because you're in distress. Let's get an understanding of the type of relationship we're going to have."

It is interesting to note that the first offer they made to Jephthah was only to be the captain of their army. This was in spite of the fact that they had previously agreed among themselves that whoever would lead them in battle would also be made the head of all Gilead (Judg. 10:18). Once Jephthah boldly stated that he wanted to understand the relationship that they now wanted, they sweetened the pot and offered him the headship of all Gilead.

I see a type of Jesus in Jephthah's dealings with his estranged brothers. Many of us only want Jesus to be our Savior, but as Jephthah wanted to be more than a captain, so Jesus does not just want to save us from eternal damnation; He wants to be our Lord! He wants to rule our lives.

This story lets us know that God does not require us to put ourselves in the position to be hurt twice. Many times when a trust has been breached, we need to forgive and exercise wisdom in how we go forward. There are people in my life with whom I know not to share confidential information;

my interaction with them is limited to certain activities and surface conversations. However, I still love them and desire to be in relationship with them on some level.

Many of us put ourselves in the position to be hurt twice, like the man who went to the doctor for a severe burn on his right cheek. The doctor asked, "How did this happen?" The man explained, "I was ironing and watching television when the phone rang. I picked up the iron instead of the phone." "I see," replied the still puzzled doctor. "But how did you get the burn on the left cheek?" he quizzed. "He called back!" the man exclaimed. This man did not learn after his first encounter with the iron. He went right ahead and did the same thing again. Jephthah didn't do this; he responded wisely to his brothers so that he would not be hurt by them again. Now, the situation with the iron may seem somewhat silly, but that is what we essentially do to ourselves when we allow someone to hurt us twice.

Lesson Three:

Man does not determine our destiny. Even though Jephthah's brothers proclaimed that he would never have an inheritance among the Gileadites, we find them *"in process of time"* (Judg. 11:4 KJV) begging Jephthah to come back. The world has a saying: "It's not over until the fat lady sings." Trust me, dear friend, men may pronounce what you can't be or won't do until they are blue in the face, but God has the last word. *"For I know the thoughts that I think toward you, saith the LORD, thoughts of peace, and not of evil, to give you an **expected end**"* (Jer. 29:11 KJV, author's emphasis).

Lesson Four:

A unity walk requires unity talk. Judges 11:12 shows that Jephthah immediately accepted the new relationship.

In contacting his enemies, he referred to the land of the Gileadites as *my* land. His history in Gilead had been interrupted by his rejection, but that was all behind him now. He fully embraced the cause. He was ready to walk in unity. A unity walk required unity talk.

Have you ever noticed how some members refer to the activities and programs of their church as events that "they" are sponsoring rather than "we"? Or what about wives who refer to their children as "my son" or "my daughter" rather than "our"? Are you one of these people? You'd be surprised at the impact that unity talk will have on your own attitude. You'll find yourself being less critical and more tolerant once you make such "team talk" a habit.

JACOB VERSUS ESAU: BUYING FORGIVENESS

My next example of the importance of forgiveness is the story of how Jacob and his scheming mother, Rebekah, conspired to cheat Esau out of the birthright due to him as the firstborn twin. Because Jacob was Rebekah's favorite, she devised a plan to trick their ailing father, Isaac, into giving the blessing to Jacob. Ironically, it was Jacob's divine destiny to receive the blessing anyway. Furthermore, Esau, in a fit of hunger, had already sold his birthright to Jacob for a bowl of lentil stew (Gen. 25:34). But Rebekah was not content to stand by and let God bring His will to pass His way; she had to assist Him. When Esau discovered the deception, he was furious.

> *Esau held a grudge against Jacob because of the blessing his father had given him. He said to himself, "The days of mourning for my father are near; then I will kill my brother Jacob." When Rebekah was told what her older son Esau had said, she sent for her younger son*

Jacob and said to him, "Your brother Esau is consoling himself with the thought of killing you. Now then, my son, do what I say: Flee at once to my brother Laban in Haran. Stay with him for a while until your brother's fury subsides. When your brother is no longer angry with you and forgets what you did to him, I'll send word for you to come back from there. Why should I lose both of you in one day?"   *(Gen. 27:41–45 NIV)*

Esau's response is not surprising when we consider the gravity of the situation; this would affect the rest of his life. In his anger, he could only speak of killing his brother. After all, hurting people, hurt people.

Rebekah, with her limited knowledge of human behavior, naively believed that the matter would blow over soon. So she shipped Jacob off to his Uncle Laban. But Jacob could not escape the law of sowing and reaping. In Haran, he worked seven years to marry his uncle's youngest daughter only to be deceived into marrying the older daughter. He was forced to work an additional seven years before his dream was fulfilled. He was also subject to numerous other deceptions. But he prospered anyway; after all, he had received Esau's blessing.

After many years, the Lord told Jacob to go back home and that He would deal well with him there. Jacob, knowing that Esau still had to be upset with him, prepared a generous peace offering consisting of numerous cattle. Then he headed home. En route, he sent messengers to tell Esau that he was on the way and had lots of presents for him. The messengers returned and advised Jacob that Esau and four hundred of his men were coming to meet him. They would arrive tomorrow. We can imagine the anxiety that Jacob must have experienced. "Will he avenge the wrong that I perpetrated upon him? Will he receive me? What will he do?"

God is faithful. Jacob had an encounter with an angel of God that night who changed Jacob's name and his nature. His new name was Israel, and he was no longer a trickster! Now Esau arrived.

> *Esau asked, "What do you mean by all these droves I met?" "To find favor in your eyes, my lord," he said. But Esau said, "I already have plenty, my brother. Keep what you have for yourself." "No, please!" said Jacob. "If I have found favor in your eyes, accept this gift from me. For to see your face is like seeing the face of God, now that you have received me favorably. Please accept the present that was brought to you, for God has been gracious to me and I have all I need." And because Jacob insisted, Esau accepted it.* (Gen. 33:8–11 NIV)

Notice that Jacob never said, "I'm sorry that I stole your birthright. Please forgive me." He did not formally apologize. He basically said, "If you're not still upset with me, accept my gifts." We must realize that some offenders may never offer the apology that we want in the manner that we desire. If reconciliation is our goal, then we'll have to do as Esau did and accept their indirect efforts. You'll just have to give up the wishful thinking.

Many men will buy their wives a gift or do something extra nice rather than apologize. Once, while conducting a marriage seminar, I asked for a show of hands from the women as to how many would prefer an apology rather than a present. The majority of the hands went up. I then asked how many would prefer an apology and a present. It was unanimous!

I know two neighbors who experienced a major rift in their relationship when one of the neighbors offended the other's wife. The offending neighbor made several attempts to express his contrition to them, but all to no avail.

In my effort to reconcile them, I asked the offended neighbor, "Hasn't he come over and asked for forgiveness?" "Oh yes, he has," he replied, "but he has not apologized. Therefore, I can't forgive him." Now here was someone who would only be satisfied with hearing a certain set of specific words. As people of God, we must grow up and exercise some spiritual maturity. We can't control what others do; we can only control our response. Furthermore, if we must insist that someone apologize to us in a certain way, then we need to let them know specifically what we want. Holding a grudge is like holding a hot coal; it will keep burning you until you let it go.

JOSEPH VERSUS HIS REPENTANT BROTHERS: "I WON'T TAKE GOD'S JOB"

I'm sure that every former Sunday school student knows the story of Joseph. There are many lessons to be learned from his life of adversity and his corresponding attitude. His example of forgiveness tops the list.

> And Joseph returned into Egypt, he, and his brethren, and all that went up with him to bury his father, after he had buried his father. And when Joseph's brethren saw that their father was dead, they said, Joseph will peradventure hate us, and will certainly requite us all the evil which we did unto him. And they sent a messenger unto Joseph, saying, Thy father did command before he died, saying, So shall ye say unto Joseph, Forgive, I pray thee now, the trespass of thy brethren, and their sin; for they did unto thee evil: and now, we pray thee, forgive the trespass of the servants of the God of thy father. And Joseph wept when they spake unto him. And his brethren also went and fell down before his face; and they said, Behold, we be thy servants.

*And Joseph said unto them, Fear not: for am I in the
place of God? But as for you, ye thought evil against
me; but God meant it unto good, to bring to pass, as it
is this day, to save much people alive. Now therefore
fear ye not: I will nourish you, and your little ones.
And he comforted them, and spake kindly unto them.*
(Gen. 50:14–21 KJV)

Joseph had settled in his spirit long ago the fact that
vengeance is God's job. In spite of all the inequities perpetrated upon him, he never sought to avenge a wrong. From
the time that he was sold away from his father at the ten-
der age of seventeen until he came into power in Egypt, he
humbly submitted to divine providence. He believed, as we
must, that all things done to us or against us—even the in-
tentional evil deeds—will eventually work for our good.
Therefore, he had no intentions of taking God's job by re-
taliating.

For those who would dare to go to another level when
following God, it is not enough to refuse to retaliate, but
we must be willing to treat the offender like an enemy.
Yes, that's right—like an enemy: *"But I say unto you, **Love**
your enemies, **bless** them that curse you, **do good** to them
that hate you, and **pray** for them which despitefully use
you, and persecute you"* (Matt. 5:44 KJV, author's emphasis).

Are you willing to love, bless, do good to, and pray for
those who have wronged you? Are you willing to be made
willing?

One of my spiritual mentors was counseling me one
day about forgiving a certain sister against whom I was
harboring some real resentment. She looked me in the eyes
and said, "Deborah, you need to make her a real target of
prayer, for there is no way that you can harbor resentment
against anyone whom you are constantly interceding for

and asking God to bless and prosper." She was right. Today, that sister and I are very close friends.

FOCUSING ON THE FUTURE

One morning I was speeding down the Pasadena freeway on my way to a workshop. I was so focused on trying to get there on time, that I did not notice the highway patrol officer on the motorcycle behind me, that is, until he sounded his siren. When I pulled over, he asked, "Don't you ever look back? I've been following you for quite some time." I explained that I was so preoccupied with trying to get to the workshop and with some other stress-inducing challenges I was facing, that I didn't realize I was speeding. After my tearful plea for mercy, he admonished me to slow down, and he let me go without a citation. Thank you, Lord!

As I reflected on this incident later, the Lord began to speak to my heart about not looking back. Looking back can be a positive thing when our objective for doing so is to get useful information that will benefit the present. David took a positive look back before he slew Goliath.

> But David said to Saul, "Your servant used to keep his father's sheep, and when a lion or a bear came and took a lamb out of the flock, I went out after it and struck it, and delivered the lamb from its mouth; and when it arose against me, I caught it by its beard, and struck and killed it. Your servant has killed both lion and bear; and this uncircumcised Philistine will be like one of them, seeing he has defied the armies of the living God."
> (1 Sam. 17:34–36)

If we're going to look back, then we must be sure that our purpose in doing so is to get useful information, to rehearse a victory, or to remember a lesson learned. Looking back should instill faith and courage to face the present.

On that freeway that morning, I could have looked back to see if it was safe to change lanes. But since I was already in the fast lane and had planned to stay there until the end of the freeway, there was no need to look back. Looking back to bemoan the fact that I had just come through some unusually heavy traffic or to get another glimpse of the driver who had cut me off earlier, would have impeded my progress or may have even caused me to wreck into something in front of me.

The Holy Spirit began to show me that this is how a lot of us live. We're on the freeway of life, and instead of focusing on the future, we're constantly looking back. We're not looking to learn or benefit from what we've come through; we're just lamenting the fact that whatever happened in the past happened to us. We ask, "Why me, Lord?" Before we know it, we have wrecked the future. Let's take a lesson from the automakers. Haven't you noticed that your windshield is a lot larger than your rearview mirror? That's because we're supposed to spend more time looking forward than back!

The apostle Paul, refusing to look back, proclaimed,

Brethren, I count not myself to have apprehended: but this one thing I do, forgetting those things which are behind, and reaching forth unto those things which are before, I press toward the mark for the prize of the high calling of God in Christ Jesus.

(Phil. 3:13–14 KJV)

Remember Lot's wife? When God decided to destroy Sodom and Gomorrah for their wickedness, he sent angels to warn Lot and his family to get out of town. Their directives were very clear:

And it came to pass, when they had brought them forth abroad, that he said, Escape for thy life; look not behind thee, neither stay thou in all the plain; escape to the mountain, lest thou be consumed....But his wife looked back from behind him, and she became a pillar of salt.
                                        (Gen. 19:17, 26 KJV)

Mrs. Lot disobeyed a direct angelic order; as a result, she became frozen in her "look back" stage. I'm sure that all of us know at least one person whose conversation indicates that he or she is stuck in the past. The tragedy is that a lot of these people are Christians. No one enjoys their company. In fact, most of their close relatives and friends look for ways to shorten their visits with them. If you are one of these people, take heed of yourself now. Stop rehearsing the ills and inequities of the past. Ask God to help you focus on your future. You are not an eternal victim. Everything that has happened to you was allowed by God for your ultimate good. Although you may never comprehend it all, believe the promise that God spoke through the prophet Jeremiah: *"For I know the thoughts that I think toward you, says the LORD, thoughts of peace and not of evil, to give you a future and a hope"* (Jer. 29:11).

If you are still alive—I assume you are, if you are reading this—you have not finished your assignment here on this earth. You still have work to do. Come on, focus on the future. Don't allow the past to make you bitter.

I am awed by the account of the three Hebrew boys, Shadrach, Meshach, and Abednego, whom King Nebuchadnezzar threw into the fiery furnace. When God delivered them out of the fire, they did not even smell like smoke (Dan. 3:27). There is a powerful lesson here. When the Hebrew boys were examined, there was no evidence that they had been in the fire. I've encountered many people who figuratively smell like smoke. Their attitude says, "I've been through the fire, and I'm upset with the world about it." They are the nasty retail clerks, the insensitive nurses, the mean ushers at church. What about you? Do you smell like smoke? Do you show evidence that you have been through the fire?

Some of us are bound by memories of the past. We replay the tapes daily. Someone once told me a story about a circus elephant. A curious patron asked the animal manager how such a huge animal could be kept under control by being chained to a stake in the ground; he could easily pop the chain with minimal effort. "But sir, you don't understand," the animal manager explained. "When the elephant was quite young and unaware of his true strength, he was bound with a chain that limited his mobility. He accepted this limitation as a permanent reality. So you see, sir, it's not the chain that binds him, but his memory!"

If you are bound by debilitating memories, here's the best antidote that I can offer:

> O LORD our God, masters besides You have had dominion over us; but by You only we make mention of Your name. They are dead, they will not live; they are deceased, they will not rise. Therefore You have punished and destroyed them, and made all their memory to perish. (Isa. 26:13–14)

Whatever the haunting memory is, we must begin to declare our deliverance from its bondage. Even psychologists agree that when we speak forth positive words, we improve our mental health. The Scottish philosopher,

Thomas Carlyle, said that if you will proclaim your freedom from bondage, that bondage will vanish.

I have walked through my house and literally yelled verse fourteen until I saw a turn in my situation. I still marvel at the vast number of Christians who do not know how to use the Word of God to obtain their deliverance. Don't you know that His words have life? *"Death and life are in the power of the tongue"* (Prov. 18:21). *"Thou shalt also decree a thing, and it shall be established unto thee: and the light shall shine upon thy ways"* (Job 22:28 KJV). These words offer powerful encouragement.

YOUR CHALLENGE

I offer the following suggestions for being able to forgive and then looking to the future. You don't need to be stuck in the past, dwelling on offenses that have been done to you. Use these suggestions to get unstuck!

- Put your tongue on a positive confession consecration for the next twenty-one days. According to experts, after this period of time a habit should be established. Refuse to discuss any injustice or hurt from the past. Make yourself accountable to a close friend or relative. Please do not select anyone who has this same problem; negativity is contagious! And for goodness' sake, try to avoid those with whom you normally commiserate. If avoiding such a one is not possible, invite him or her to join you in your consecration. Replace every negative thought with a promise from God's Word.

- Begin to talk about and plan things you'd like to do. Start with a small project or activity and assign a due date to it. Goals without due dates are just wishes. Here are some suggestions to get you started: plan a twenty-minute walk with someone three days a week, invite a few people over for a short prayer meeting or Sunday dinner within the next two weeks, or visit a hospice in the next few weeks. The list is endless. You just need to get unstuck. Unlike Lot's wife, you still have that option.

Forgiveness is simply releasing the desire to see the wrong avenged. As I have said, holding on to a hurt or an offense is like holding a hot coal; the longer you hold it, the more it harms you. Let it go. You can do it with the help of the Holy Spirit. Remember, it's God who works in you to will and to do of His good pleasure.

Part IV

CAPE Personality Styles

Chapter Thirteen

Determining Personality Temperament

The major problems experienced by most organizations are not technology related, but are rooted in how people deal with each other. While every person is different, people are motivated by common fears and needs. Conflicts arise when these fears are tapped into or needs are unmet.

At the beginning of the book I explained the four basic styles of managing conflict and confrontation. In this section, I will explore four basic personality temperaments that most of us reflect, not only in conflict, but also in our day-to-day interactions with others. These temperaments closely parallel how we choose to handle conflict.

To get started, you need to determine your own personality temperament. Answer the questions on the following

pages as honestly and quickly as possible. When done, simply tally the number of *Yes* responses for each personality
style. Then, depending on the number of *Yes* responses for
each page, you can determine how your personality fits
into the profiles that make up the acronym CAPE, which I
will discuss in the next chapter.

Determining Personality Temperament

THE "C" PERSONALITY QUIZ

Indicate Yes or No to each of the questions below:

_____ 1. Do you have a strong need to be in control?

_____ 2. Are you decisive?

_____ 3. Do others look to you to be the leader in most situations?

_____ 4. Are you direct and to the point in interactions with others?

_____ 5. Are you intolerant of the weaknesses, short-comings, or annoying mannerisms of others?

_____ 6. Do you judge people by their productivity or their ability to get things done quickly?

_____ 7. Are you usually right?

_____ 8. Do you have difficulty admitting you're wrong?

_____ 9. Do you often choose work over relaxing or so-cializing with family or friends?

_____ 10. Do you find that you sometimes, unintention-ally, offend people?

Total number of *Yes* responses: _____

The "A" Personality Quiz

Indicate Yes or No to each of the questions below:

_____1. Are you warm, friendly, and outgoing?

_____2. Do you often initiate conversation with strangers?

_____3. Are you usually the first to volunteer to help someone in distress?

_____4. Are you a good encourager?

_____5. Do you tend to be disorganized or to lose things often?

_____6. Do most people like you and desire your company?

_____7. Are you good on stage?

_____8. Are you able to find humor in most situations?

_____9. Do you tend not to pay close attention to details?

_____10. Do you tend to tolerate poor performance from others for too long?

Total number of *Yes* responses: _____

Determining Personality Temperament

THE "P" PERSONALITY QUIZ

Indicate Yes or No to each of the questions below:

_____1. Are you reliable?

_____2. Do you prefer not to lead in most endeavors?

_____3. Do you usually maintain an unhurried pace?

_____4. Are you a good listener?

_____5. Are you good under pressure?

_____6. Do you find that you prefer the status quo and thus are likely to resist change?

_____7. Do you find it hard to get motivated to pursue a goal?

_____8. Are you a team player?

_____9. Do you tend to look for the easy way to do things?

_____10. Do you prefer to avoid conflict and confrontation?

Total number of *Yes* responses: _____

THE "E" PERSONALITY QUIZ

Indicate Yes or No to each of the questions below:

_____1. Do you require precision and accuracy in things you do?

_____2. Are you neat and organized?

_____3. Do you often give detailed explanations?

_____4. Do you tend to overanalyze data before making a decision?

_____5. Do people perceive you as "serious"?

_____6. Are you cautious in establishing new friend-ships?

_____7. Do you enjoy or prefer difficult work?

_____8. Are you content to stay in the background?

_____9. Do you feel compelled to finish what you start?

_____10. Do you prefer to avoid personal confrontation?

Total number of *Yes* responses: _____

Determining Personality Temperament

PERSONALITY STYLE ASSESSMENT

Summarize below the number of *Yes* responses from each personality quiz:

"C" Personality Quiz   _____

"A" Personality Quiz   _____

"P" Personality Quiz   _____

"E" Personality Quiz   _____

According to this test, what is your dominant personality temperament (highest single number above)?

_____

What is your secondary (five *Yes* responses or more) temperament?

_____

Note: If you answered yes to a majority (six or more) of the questions on more than two of the personality tests, this could be an indication that you are trying to be "all things to all men" (1 Cor. 9:22), but not in the positive way that the apostle Paul recommended. You may be attempting to meet the expectations of too many people or are unclear as to what others expect from you in your present environment. Obviously such behavior can cause a great deal of stress and may lead to related illnesses. Take a quiet moment and ask God if this is so.

Hippocrates first introduced the four temperaments hundreds of years before Jesus was born. He called them the Choleric, the Sanguine, the Phlegmatic, and the Melancholy. Most people find these descriptions intimidating and too hard to remember. Therefore, I asked the Holy Spirit for a simple method of identifying and remembering these personality types. Thus the CAPE Personality Profile was born. Each personality type is likened to the categories of individuals found on an airline flight:

C-Captain (Choleric)

A-Flight Attendant (Sanguine)

P-Passenger (Phlegmatic)

E-Flight Engineer (Melancholy)

Note: I interviewed several airline pilots for this section and was informed that the position of flight engineer is currently found only on 727s, DC-10s, and older 747 airplanes. A computer now performs this function on the newer planes. Notwithstanding, the Engineer function describes one of the four personality styles or temperaments.

Chapter Fourteen

Defining Personality Styles

As we examine all the personality styles, you will learn how to capitalize on your strengths and to appreciate the strengths that others bring to the table. You will also be challenged to face your weaknesses and to be more tolerant of the weaknesses of others.

THE CAPTAIN

The Captain is the one who must be in control of the aircraft. He is the leader of the crew. The buck stops with him. He must pilot the plane to its final destination. Therefore, he is more task oriented than people oriented. This is not to say that the Captain doesn't desire to interact with others, but, given the option, he makes the task his top priority. We find the Captain interacting one-on-one with the passengers and saying good-bye after the plane has landed. The mission has been accomplished.

One of the Captain's greatest personality strengths is that he is decisive. In turbulent conditions, he decides when the seat belt light will be turned on and off. He decides when the plane should go to another altitude to avoid turbulence. He can perform many functions and is not overwhelmed by a heavy workload. The Captain is always the leader or the perceived leader. He will embrace a new challenge like a teddy bear. Look at Joshua and Caleb's response to the giants whom they and the other ten spies saw in the Promised Land.

And Joshua the son of Nun, and Caleb the son of Jephunneh, which were of them that searched the land, rent their clothes: and they spake unto all the company of the children of Israel, saying, The land, which we passed through to search it, is an exceeding good land. If the LORD delight in us, then he will bring us into this land, and give it us; a land which floweth with milk and honey. (Num. 14:6–8 KJV)

Joshua and Caleb were real Captains. They were willing to trust God and step out in faith. Captains are courageous and motivational. They have low regard for those who procrastinate or who do not finish a task. Captains are not long-suffering with the shortcomings, incompetence, or weaknesses of others. The apostle Paul, a New Testament Captain, showed his intolerance by refusing to take John Mark on a second missionary trip after Mark had left him and Barnabas high and dry on the first trip (Acts 15:36–40).

My friend Esther Eutsey is over seventy years old and has a real Captain's personality. She is as direct in her communication style as they come. She is multitalented and works very fast. Recently, she assisted me in a special project by inserting the ribbons in some specialty bookmarks that we were developing. I was not home when she dropped off the finished product; however, she had done a great job. Incidentally, I have had such wonderful experiences with senior citizens. They are among the most thorough and dependable workers around.

Because of my traveling schedule, I did not call her for several weeks after the project. But Captain Esther was not going to sit around and wonder for long what I thought about the quality of her work. After a couple of weeks, she left the following message on my answering machine. "Hello. This is Esther Eutsey. I have not heard from you since I did those ribbons. Did I mess them up? Call me!"

A typical Captain. They like to know how they're doing so that they can stay in control of the situation. They do not run from confrontation. While the Captain welcomes confrontation, he is the least likely of all the temperaments to be confronted since he has the most intimidating, dominant personality.

When in doubt about performance on or off the job, the Captain will ask for input or evaluation. Why ponder the situation and assume the worst? You may not be as bold as my friend Esther, but at least you could ask, "Do you have any suggestions on how I could improve my performance or how I could have resolved that problem more effectively?"

In a conflict, a Captain will often use a Dictator approach in order to resolve the issue. After all, Captains are usually right. Unfortunately, they often forget that they are not *always* right. Notwithstanding, a Captain is open to a win-win negotiation but will resist generalizations or statements made without support. The opponent or one who confronts him must get to the point quickly and not circle the airport with long, detailed explanations. The Captain must land the plane—now!

The one who confronts a Captain must also show respect for the Captain's authority. Since the Captain's greatest fear is the fear of losing control, he does not respond well when one challenges his authority or goes over his head. Of course, the Captain could help to insure harmony by being less dictatorial and domineering. He must learn to acknowledge the fact that God has given everyone something of value to bring to the table. By managing his impatience, he will begin to listen, without interruption, to the opinions or desires of others, even if they are presented in a long-drawn-out manner.

Finally, the Captain must learn to respect the boundaries of others. He must stop trying to fix every problem he observes. He must abandon his sacred belief that "the Captain knows best."

THE ATTENDANT

Flight attendants' primary focus is the comfort and safety of the passengers. They greet each passenger at the entrance to the plane and create a friendly atmosphere. They make conversations with complete strangers. Attendants show interest in whatever the stranger wants to discuss. They make every effort to respond to the needs of passengers. In an emergency, the flight attendant is the first to move into action on behalf of the passengers.

Attendants are always volunteering: "Would you like a drink?" "Blankets, anyone?" Often they forget to bring the extra pillow or blanket that one passenger requested because they are so busy accommodating another. They tend to overcommit themselves. My husband and I have a friend who stays in trouble with his wife because he is always rescuing a damsel or anybody else in distress. He forgets that he has promised to be home at a certain time for a planned activity. He sincerely enjoys helping others, and everyone loves him. However, his wife just doesn't always appreciate his overcommitment to others.

Defining Personality Styles

Flight attendants desire to leave a good impression on the passengers so that they continue to patronize their particular airline. The Attendant's greatest fear is the loss of social approval or fear of rejection. In managing conflict, the Attendant will normally take the Accommodator approach. In an earlier chapter, we saw Peter straddle the fence in his attempt to befriend Gentiles and Jews. Captain Paul, knowing what was best, confronted him about his hypocrisy (Gal. 2:11–14). Aaron chose to accommodate the wishes of the Israelites in the wilderness and built a golden calf (Exod. 32:4). Certain chief rulers chose not to accept Jesus as the Messiah for fear of alienation by their peers (John 12:42). All of these Attendant personalities share a common thread: they all feared the loss of social approval.

The other personality styles often view those with the Attendant temperament as flighty, superficial, and desiring the spotlight, since they are so good with people and are comfortable at center stage. Remember that our opinions are not facts. We must accept the Attendant the way that God has made him.

While understanding the fear of the Attendant, those in conflict or the one who confronts the Attendant should be careful to let the Attendant know that only his behavior is being rejected or called into question. The approach must be caring and supportive, while establishing clear goals and boundaries. When Jesus confronted the woman caught in adultery, His approach was filled with compassion. However, He admonished her to *"go and sin no more"* (John 8:11). We must be very clear with Attendants on what must be done and the timeline for doing it. Most importantly, we must express our commitment to continue the relationship.

Attendants would do well in their efforts to maintain harmony and effectiveness by being less tolerant of the mediocre performance of others. Ironically, this very be-havior often causes some, especially Captains, to begin to resent, lose respect for, and reject the Attendant. It be-comes the paradox bemoaned by Job: *"For the thing which I greatly feared is come upon me, and that which I was afraid of is come unto me."* (Job 3:25 KJV)

THE PASSENGER

The passengers are the ones who participate passively in the flight. They do not get involved in the operation of the aircraft. They may have strong opinions about the flight, but in most instances, they do not confront the Cap-tain. Passengers may even have questions but will either refrain from asking the flight attendant or will opt to ask another passenger. On a recent flight to Minneapolis, the head flight attendant announced that the à la carte dinner service was about to start. I overheard one passenger ask another, "What's à la carte?" I waited carefully to see if ei-ther of them would ask the flight attendant to explain when they were served. They both kept quiet.

Passengers do as they are told. They buckle their seat belts and return their seat backs to the upright position for take off and landing. Passengers do not like change with regard to the flight: no delays, no cancellations, no running out of the food entrées, and please no turbulence. They prefer the status quo; the flight should depart and arrive as originally established. Everything should go smoothly.

The majority of the individuals on any flight are the passengers. The majority of people in life are Passengers. There are only a few Captains or leaders. This is all part of God's divine purpose. Imagine all chiefs and no Indians, or all Indians and no chiefs. Would any purpose ever get ac-complished?

Before we disdain Passengers, let's look at the strengths of this personality temperament. Passengers are good at reconciling conflicts between others because they believe so strongly in peace and harmony. Passengers are loyal and dependable. They are needed to accomplish goals and objectives. Without passengers, airlines could not remain in business. Factories and other businesses would have no one to perform the routine, day-to-day operations. The Passengers prefer routine. They are the backbone of organized labor. Passengers are team players. In a crisis, they are capable of coming through. How many acts of passenger heroism have we read about when a plane has crashed?

Of course, the Passenger temperament has its weaknesses. Passengers prefer to maintain the status quo. Their greatest fear is the loss of security. They are the primary focus of all political campaigns since they represent the masses. The politicians promise security and stability. Passengers buy the promise. When Passengers feel betrayed, they get even by quietly voting to throw the bums out.

We see the Passenger temperament in action with the Israelites after the Exodus from Egypt. On several occasions they reminded Moses that he should have maintained the status quo. The first time was when they felt trapped between Pharaoh's pursuing army and the Red Sea.

As Pharaoh approached, the Israelites looked up, and there were the Egyptians, marching after them. They were terrified and cried out to the LORD. They said to Moses, "Was it because there were no graves in Egypt that you brought us to the desert to die? What have you done to us by bringing us out of Egypt? Didn't we say to you in Egypt, 'Leave us alone; let us serve the Egyptians'? It would have been better for us to serve the Egyptians than to die in the desert!"

(Exod. 14:10–12 NIV)

They would subsequently remind him on several other occasions that he should have just let things be. Passengers will not normally volunteer for leadership. They'll murmur that somebody should do something.

> *And wherefore hath the LORD brought us unto this land, to fall by the sword, that our wives and our children should be a prey? were it not better for us to return into Egypt? And they said one to another, Let us make a captain, and let us return into Egypt.*
>
> (Num. 14:3–4 KJV)

By default, Passengers cause Captains to assume their role. As a confessed Captain, I have often tried to resist taking the lead so that I could allow others to do so—all to no avail. Passengers like to be led. They are not self-motivated enough to achieve goals on their own. They must be wound up and put on the track, so to speak, if they are to get going.

Passengers hate confrontation. Therefore, in a conflict, Passengers may take the Abdicator approach. They may just retreat, usually emotionally rather than physically. After all, Passengers do not like change. They will stay in a relationship longer than any other personality group, just to maintain the status quo.

In a personal conflict with a Passenger, one must be on guard not to push too hard. He must express sincere appreciation for whatever the Passenger has accomplished. The sandwich approach discussed earlier is a must. Remember: bread (appreciation), then meat (the problem), and more bread (appreciation).

Even though the Passenger personality may believe that you care, he still may not respond as quickly as one, especially a Captain, would desire. We must be careful not to judge the Passenger as a passive, apathetic, low achiever. He will get the job done, but he is more relationship oriented than task oriented.

THE ENGINEER

The flight engineer is the crew member who is responsible for the mechanical performance of the aircraft in flight. His job requires much attention to detail, and this job is critical to a successful flight. He will not be found socializing with the passengers. His focus in on the instrument panel, cabin pressurization, fuel usage, and other operating systems. He must be a perfectionist in interpreting the readings. Imagine if he were to respond to a malfunctioning gauge with, "Oh, it doesn't seem too bad." The passengers' safety would be jeopardized!

The strength of the Engineer is that he is very analytical. He will tend to choose a profession that the average person finds too difficult. He sets high standards for himself and others. The Engineer spouse will redo the dishes or other household job after the other spouse has finished the task. In learning to maintain harmony, we understand that the Engineer simply has a need for things to be done precisely. The Engineer must learn to let some things go.

My husband and I jokingly refer to each other as "Oscar" (me) and "Felix" (him) from the television sitcom *The Odd Couple*. Felix was very neat and conscientious, while Oscar was quite messy. To minimize conflict in our household on this issue, we've each learned to give a little. I don't leave my high heels at the door, so he has stopped tripping—literally! He gives me a thirty-minute warning before he comes home each day so that I have time to tidy whatever needs to be tidied. We have discussed what annoys him most, and I focus on those areas primarily. I'm actually a lot neater now, but it seems like nothing when compared with his neatness.

Engineers are not quick to make a decision. They will analyze a problem to death. They will agonize over the simplest issue. What will I order to eat? Which car do I really like best? On and on it goes. They drive the decisive Captain crazy! And of course, Engineers are very rules and regulations oriented. They will rarely ask to be the exception to a policy.

Esther, the Jewish queen of Persia, had an Engineer temperament. Her cousin Mordecai informed her that the Jews were about to be exterminated through wicked Haman's plot to destroy all the Jews, which was a result of Mordecai's refusal to pay him honor. Mordecai wanted her to go to the king, her husband, to plead for the life of her people. Her first response was that such an act would be against the law, or company policy, so to speak:

> *All the king's servants and the people of the king's provinces know that any man or woman who goes into the inner court to the king, who has not been called, he has but one law: put all to death, except the one to whom the king holds out the golden scepter, that he may live. Yet I myself have not been called to go in to the king these thirty days.* (Est. 4:11)

After much fasting and praying, Esther decided to go to the king in spite of the law, and she risked her life in doing so. *"I will go to the king, which is against the law; and if I perish, I perish!"* (v. 16). Having found favor with the king, she didn't rush to tell him the reason for her coming. She invited him and Haman to dinner. At the dinner, she promised to tell him at a follow-up dinner on the next day what she really wanted. Now, had Esther been a Captain, she would have told him the minute he extended the golden scepter. But no, Engineers are thorough and systematic in their approach to conflict resolution and problem solving. It was at the second dinner that she exposed Haman's plot, and the Jews were saved from death.

Let's learn to appreciate the thoroughness of Engineers. They take great care to be correct, to be right. Their decisions are not based on emotions, but on facts and verifiable data. Consequently, their greatest fear is the fear of criticism. After all, they take such great pains to be right. Engineers provide the balance that is needed for the overly optimistic Attendant and the sometimes too-hasty Captain. One must be careful to listen to the logic of the Engineer; the Engineer must learn when enough analysis is enough. Sometimes, he just has to step out in faith as Esther did.

In summary, when in conflict with the Engineer, one must have his facts straight. Allow plenty of time, if possible, for his questions, doubts, and concerns about the issue. Give concrete reasons why you oppose them. Attempts to persuade him with emotions or people-centered arguments will yield few results. He is task oriented, and things must make sense. The best cure for a life that always needs to make sense is to saturate one's spirit with the promises of God. Engineers will often find it hard to walk by faith and may miss some of the blessings that only come by stepping out in reliance on God's promises.

SUMMARY

The foregoing discussion was not intended to put anyone in a box from which there is no escape. It is merely a tool for understanding our own needs and fears and those of others. We can then equip ourselves to interact harmoniously with people of different temperaments. Also, we should be cautioned to remember that almost no one is any single style. Most of us are a blend of styles. No single behavioral style is better or worse than the other; therefore, one style should not be exalted above another. Be careful not to immediately categorize a person based on your observation of a single action. Sometimes the situation will dictate an individual's behavior. In a crisis, we may see an Attendant personality become a Captain and demand the necessary actions to resolve the problem. Therefore, it is important to look for consistent behavior over a period of time before attempting to attribute a certain personality style to anyone.

Of course, we may all believe from time to time that we'd have fewer problems if everyone were just like us. Give up the wishful thinking. Learn to accept and appreciate the differences in others. In doing so, we will enhance our interactions with others and find that harmony can be achieved.

YOUR CHALLENGE

Write the name of one person for each relationship listed below. For each person, indicate one strategy that you can begin to employ immediately to be more effective in your interactions with him or her.

Name   **Strategy**

(Example)

Dorothy   *I will patiently listen to her detailed explanations without interruption.*

Defining Personality Styles

Friend:

_____   _____

Relative:

_____   _____

Coworker:

_____   _____

Other:

_____   _____

Which personality style do you enjoy interacting with the most? Why?

_____

_____

Which personality style do you have the most difficulty dealing with? Why?

_____

_____

What weaknesses in your own personality are you now willing to put on the altar?

_____

_____

Part V

Confrontation Guidelines for Specific Situations

Chapter Fifteen

Family Relationships

In my confrontation seminars, we have role-playing to allow the participants to practice their newfound skills in confronting issues. In this chapter and the ones following, I've included some common situations that crop up in our daily interactions and some suggested guidelines for confronting them. In this chapter, I will present some situations that relate to family relationships. Of course, this chapter will not be able to cover every conflict that may arise in a family, but the tips presented here may help in many different family conflicts.

SITUATION: THE UNSUPPORTIVE HUSBAND

Your husband works hard at his office each day. You also work hard each day, whether at the office or at home.

When he comes home, he grabs the sports section of the newspaper and waits for you to finish making dinner. You help little Johnny with his homework after you finish the dishes. You go to bed dead tired while your husband settles in to watch the late news. You really resent the fact that he won't help out. You've tolerated his insensitivity ever since Johnny was born. Tell him about it.

Resolution Guidelines:

- Don't resort to passive-aggressive behavior, that is, sulking and being moody and hoping that he'll figure out what's wrong.

- Tell him how much you appreciate what he does already, for example, being financially responsible, and so forth. Use lots of bread in the confrontation "sandwich." Most men respond to appreciation.

- Don't attack him for being insensitive. By doing everything yourself in the past, you may have taught him that it was okay not to help. He's not a mind reader.

- Give him options on specific tasks—washing dishes, bathing the child, doing laundry, or paying bills—so that he doesn't feel you're being a dictator.

- Acknowledge and express appreciation for any noticed improvements.

SITUATION: SIBLINGS SHARING MOM'S BURDEN

Your aging mother divorced your father many years ago. Her monthly social security check is not sufficient to cover all of her current financial requirements. You have four siblings, three of whom are very responsible, although not as successful as you, the attorney. Your brother, Ron, does odd jobs from time to time but is supported primarily by his girlfriend with whom he lives.

You have called the rest of your siblings with a request for support for your mother. Everyone, except Ron, has agreed to $150 per month. Ron says that he can't commit to a definite amount because his earnings are sporadic. He says that whenever he has a little extra money, he'll take it to her.

You disapprove of every aspect of Ron's life. You wonder if he will ever grow up. You're feeling angry that his commitment is so vague. You've decided that he must commit to something more definite. You call him back.

Resolution Guidelines:

- Maintain a positive attitude. Do not refer to his irresponsibility or to his lifestyle. Stick to the issue at hand.

- Ask him what minimum financial commitment he could make for the official support-money pool.

- Try to negotiate a non-financial commitment. For example, since his schedule is flexible, ask him if he would be willing to take her to the doctor or to run other errands two days a week.

- Don't brag or whine that you will be required to cover the lion's share of the budget. He may resent you.

- Tell him how much you and his mother will appreciate whatever effort he puts forth.

SITUATION: THE HALF-TRUTH AND NOTHING BUT

Your husband, Robert, a corporate manager, told you that he was taking Jim and Molly to lunch to show his appreciation for their assistance to his department during a recent government audit. You thought nothing of it until later when he mentioned that the service had been good, and that the *four* of them had thoroughly enjoyed the food. With your normal curiosity, you asked who the fourth person was. He sheepishly admitted that his attractive assistant manager, Lula, had also joined them. Now you're upset, not because she joined them, but because Robert felt the need to hide it. Until this point in your twenty-year marriage, he has never given you a reason to doubt his integrity, but now you wonder. Robert has been caught in a half-truth.

Resolution Guidelines:

- Stay calm.

- Don't immediately accuse Robert of having an affair with Lula.

- Ask Robert why he felt the need to hide the truth. Listen carefully to his explanation.

- Ask yourself if, perhaps, you've expressed an inordinate amount of jealousy that could have caused Robert to fear your response had you known the truth.

- Let him know the impact that the lie has had upon you (for example, disappointment, slight loss of trust, etc.).

- Ask the Holy Spirit for grace to forgive him.

- Do not rehearse the incident each time Robert doesn't do what you ask.

SITUATION: THE SPENDTHRIFT TEENAGER

You give your sixteen-year-old son an allowance on the first and fifteenth of each month. Since he started dating a girl from an affluent family, he always seems to need a little extra cash prior to the next allowance date. The first couple of times he asked, you obliged him. However, you realize that you are hindering him from learning how to manage his money. You have been a good parent and prefer not to have any tension in the relationship. But love must be tough.

Resolution Guidelines:

- Tell your son, in a matter-of-fact tone, that you love him too much to continue to bridge his financial gaps.

- Stick to your guns; let him reap the consequences of overspending.

- Suggest that he find low-cost ways to entertain his new flame.

SITUATION: THE BABY-SITTING-WEARY GRANDMA

Grandma, you've just hung up from a conversation with your son, who announced that he'd be bringing the kids over for the weekend. He and his wife are going to Las Vegas to have a little fun. Last weekend his old chums from college were in town, and he needed you to baby-sit then, also. Since your husband's death, they have assumed that you have nothing else to do. You didn't mean it literally when you said you're always available. In fact, you recently joined a support group at church and have been looking forward to the planned activities. To be quite honest, you rarely have the time to baby-sit consistently. You have a life now too. Confront your son.

Resolution Guidelines:

- Express how much you love your grandchildren.

- Admit responsibility for creating the situation that is now troubling you.

- Express your intent to retire from baby-sitting except for when it's convenient for you.

- Abandon the fear that he will retaliate by refusing to let you see the grandchildren; you'll always be the most trusted baby-sitter.

Chapter Sixteen

Professional Interactions

H ere, I will present various situations that may arise in the workplace. Again, the scenarios described in this chapter cannot begin to cover all of the possible conflicts that can come up on the job, but I believe that these situations are representative of workplace conflicts. The guidelines presented in this chapter will most likely help you in certain workplace conflicts.

SITUATION: THE OVERWORKED ASSISTANT

You were recently hired to work for a small accounting firm. The pay is great, and the three partners are all wonderful Christians. Yesterday was the first day of the busy season. Each partner has given you a list of tasks to perform. Clearly, you will not be able to complete all of them in the allotted time. In addition, you won't be able to work much overtime since your husband recently had major surgery and is still immobile.

Resolution Guidelines:

- Thoroughly review the list of tasks to get an estimate of the time required to complete them.

- Ask your immediate supervisor to rank or approve your ranking of the priorities. Caution: don't get frustrated if the boss deems a task more important than you feel it should be. Submit to his or her authority.

- Be as flexible as your home life permits. If you can come in for a half-day on Saturday or work two hours extra on Wednesday, say so.

- If the busy season never seems to end, ask God to open another door of employment. Your employer is not your only source of employment, but a chosen channel for a particular season.

SITUATION: THE UNPROFESSIONAL BOSS

Your boss has no people skills. She confronts her staff openly and loudly. This is a real deal-breaker for you. Before you joined the company several months ago, you had specifically asked if employees were treated with dignity and respect. She had assured you that such was the case.

This morning at the weekly staff meeting, she had a hostile confrontation with one of the project managers. She humiliated him while the rest of the staff sat in stone silence. Recognizing her need for salvation, you have learned to look beyond her faults and see her needs. Notwithstanding, you have decided that she should be advised of how her behavior is affecting staff morale as well as the company's image.

Resolution Guidelines:

- Invite her to a private location to discuss the matter. She may become hostile and embarrass you as well. This is a real risk in confronting.

- Use the sandwich approach discussed earlier.

  > *Bread:* Tell her how much you appreciate the role that she has played in bringing the company to where it is today.

  > *Meat:* While you have not personally experienced her wrath, own the problem anyway. You may be next! Explain how you feel when another employee is humiliated. Be careful not to use judgmental statements or phrases such as "you should...."

  > *Bread:* Reaffirm your commitment to support her personally as well as to support the company objectives.

- Thank her for being willing to listen to you.

SITUATION: SHARING THE BILL

Every Friday, you and several of your coworkers go to a local restaurant for lunch. You always seem to end up paying a disproportionate share of the bill relative to your order, although the food is moderately priced. Just last week, after the tab was divided equally, your share was ten dollars. You had only ordered a three-dollar bowl of soup!

You are beginning to resent the fact that some people in the group order expensive appetizers, extra drinks, and dessert. You want to continue these get-togethers, but you'd really prefer to pay for your food separately. You've kept quiet until now for fear that the others may call you "cheap" if you were to request a separate check.

Resolution Guidelines:

- First be aware that some restaurants will not give separate checks for a party of five or more.

- Announce lightheartedly before orders are taken that you're going to be a better manager of your money and will only be spending a certain amount. Therefore, you're having the (whatever).

- When the bill arrives, be the first to place the appropriate amount, including taxes and tip, on the table. Politely ignore any subsequent attempts to saddle you with more of the bill. If you're really uncomfortable, excuse yourself from the table while the rest figure out their share of the bill.

SITUATION: PROMOTION DENIED

Your promotion or raise has been denied for three years straight. You know you're doing a good job. In fact, you've trained over half the people in your department. In addition, your husband was on strike from his job for an entire month and your savings have been depleted. You could use the extra money now. You plan to confront the boss.

Resolution Guidelines:

- Keep a personal record of your achievements on the job; refer to them when you present your request.

- Never ask for a raise based on your financial obligations; raises should be based on the value of the job and your performance.

- If your request is denied, ask for specific recommendations on what you need to do for your request to be granted later. Agree on the time period for what will be considered "later."

- Remember that, according to Psalm 75:6–7, promotion comes from God.

SITUATION: SEXUAL HARASSMENT

You are being sexually harassed by a manager from another department who is part of the good old boy's network. He plays tennis with your boss twice a week. His advances started a couple of weeks ago when he looked you up and down at the water cooler. You feel you should stop this as soon as possible before it goes any further. Confront this person who is harassing you.

Resolution Guidelines:

- Ask the Holy Spirit to give you words that will have the most impact.

- Approach him in his office while he is alone. Remain standing.

- Forget the sandwich approach, and get right to the meat of the matter.

- Start by giving this person the benefit of the doubt. "You may not be aware of it, but your behavior toward me constitutes sexual harassment." Looking directly into his eyes with a sober expression, emphatically state, "It must be stopped. If such behavior continues, I will have to report it." Use whatever specific words God has given you.

- If the harasser doesn't take you seriously, or if he attempts to minimize your concern, assure him that you will take the issue to the next level.

Chapter Seventeen

Social and Other Interactions

Finally, I will present various situations that may crop up in other areas of life. Remember, the guidelines I give here are outlines that undoubtedly will help you to handle similar situations.

SITUATION: "I HATE MY ENTRÉE"

This month's budget finally allows you to have dinner at a certain upscale restaurant. You order the day's special at the suggestion of your waiter. After the first bite of the dish, you realize that it is not what you expected. It is much too rich for your diet. You really feel bad about this because the waiter has been so nice up to this point. However, you've made a commitment to abandon your Abdicator conflict management style, so you've decided to return the entrée.

Resolution Guidelines:

- Don't delay. I know a woman who, upon consuming an entire stack of pancakes, demanded that they be taken off her check. She alleged that they were burned! The waiter was appalled that there was no evidence to support her claim.

- Quietly explain to the waiter why you are returning the dish.

- Don't attack the waiter because of your disappointment; he didn't prepare the food.

- Before you order the replacement dish, ask exactly how it is prepared.

SITUATION: THE UNGRATEFUL GUESTS

You are a budding speaker and writer, or other professional. During the past month, you attended several very expensive seminars on how to be more successful in your profession. You invite a small group of similarly aspiring individuals over to your house to share the valuable insights you have gained from the seminars. They all thank you for your kindness. However, only two of them sent a subsequent thank-you note to formally express their appreciation. You're perturbed by the lack of manners of the ones who didn't send a card.

Resolution Guidelines:

- Ask yourself what your true motive was for inviting them over. Was it to be thanked, to show off, or to share information?

- Realize that everyone doesn't share your grace or manners. It doesn't mean that they are bad or ungrateful. They probably had no intentions of offending you. Remember Proverbs 19:11: *"A man's wisdom gives him patience; it is to his glory to overlook an offense"* (NIV). So forget about it!

SITUATION: THE INCOMPETENT PASTOR

You belong to a small church that is part of a democratically run denomination. The pastor assigned to the church by headquarters is not working out. His sermons are boring and unchallenging. He has no real vision for the church or the community. Furthermore, he's in poor health.

You are a member of several prominent committees, but not the committee that would be responsible for the removal of the pastor. You have an open, honest, and supportive relationship with the pastor. However, you feel that you would incur the wrath of God for touching His anointed if you were to participate on any level in helping to get him removed.

Of course, the pastoral committee has taken an ostrich stance—burying their heads in the sand, so to speak—in addressing the issue and has joined the rest of the congregation in murmuring about his incompetence and in wishing that he would resign.

Resolution Guidelines:

- Resist the temptation to join the murmuring.

- Ask God if He is calling you to be the pastor's "Samuel" (see 1 Samuel 3:11–18) by telling him the unpleasant news.

- If God gives you the green light to discuss the matter with the pastor, own the problem. State how his performance has affected you personally, as well as how it has affected the other members.

- Don't demand his resignation. Stay in your role as a messenger.

- If the pastor doesn't resign, or you see no improvement over a reasonable period of time, look for another church. Your spiritual life is at stake.

SITUATION: THE FORNICATING DEACON

You have heard that Jim, cochairman of the deacon board, has moved in with his girlfriend. Jim has been a faithful tither and a good leader. You have noticed, however, that his attendance at the weekly deacons' meetings has been sporadic. He also seems to have lost some of his zeal for the Lord. As the pastor, you feel that you must address this matter right away to minimize further negative impact on the congregation.

Resolution Guidelines:

- Call Jim and set a time to meet with him right away.

- Don't accuse him of being guilty before you ask if the rumor is true.

- If he admits to the wrongdoing, explain to him the previously decided consequences, which should include the following: immediate relinquishment of his leadership position and submission to spiritual counseling.

Note: You may also consider requiring him to apologize to the church since the matter is public knowledge.

- Express your desire and commitment to see him restored to a right relationship with God and with the church.

SITUATION: A LEECHING FRIEND

A relative or friend has borrowed money from you and has conveniently forgotten to repay you again. You resent the fact that she lives above her means while you often forego certain pleasures to save money. She now finds herself in another financial jam and needs to "borrow a little change." You have decided to put a stop to it.

Resolution Guidelines:

- Be a broken record in saying "no."

- Realize that by always bailing the person out, you are enabling the person to remain irresponsible.

- Don't leave the door open for a future request by saying you don't have the money this time.

- Refuse to be manipulated or made to feel guilty.

SITUATION: THE IMMODEST FRIEND

Lucy accepted the Lord and joined the church last year. Since then, she and you have attended various functions together and occasionally enjoy girl talk on the phone. Lucy is a real knockout; she has it, and she flaunts it. In fact, some of her outfits are downright indecent, but she wears them to church anyway.

Needless to say, she is the focus of attention wherever she goes. Even the highly spiritual men struggle to keep from eyeing her. You feel a real burden to see her mature in the Lord and be more modest in her dress. You've decided that it's time to discuss this matter with her.

Resolution Guidelines:

- Not so fast! Have you earned the right to delve into such a sensitive area of her life? Does she know that you genuinely care?

- How much do you know about her background and any issues from her past that could have possibly caused her to feel that dressing this way is the only way to be valued?

- If you honestly feel that you have earned the right to speak of this matter, start by asking her some non-accusatory questions such as the following: "Have you noticed the impact that your presence has on the men of the church? Perhaps this is a blind spot, and I care enough to make you aware of it." Or, "How do you think God feels about how you dress? Do you acknowledge Him in this regard?"

- You may want to share a past struggle that you've overcome so that you do not come across as being self-righteous.

- You may consider giving her a book on modesty or sharing with her the Scriptures on this subject.

- Reaffirm your commitment to maintaining a mutually beneficial relationship.

Epilogue

Confrontation carries a risk. Jesus knew that when He commanded us to confront those who have wronged us. *"Moreover if thy brother shall trespass against thee, go and tell him his fault between thee and him alone: if he shall hear thee, thou hast gained thy brother. But if he will not hear thee..."* (Matt. 18:15–16 KJV).

You may follow all of the principles of effective confrontation discussed in this book and still not get the response you desire. This does not mean that the confrontation failed. Take no responsibility for someone else's response. You've planted the seed; you cannot make it grow. You've obeyed God; the rest is His job.

Once you learn to confront and stop being a victim, you will love yourself. You will stop having conversations with yourself about what you should have said or beating yourself up because you didn't speak up. You'll feel empowered. Your self-esteem will increase, and you will gain the respect of others. Notwithstanding, others may initially be put off by your new behavior.

I heard Dr. James Dobson, the popular Christian psychologist, say that he once told his outspoken son that "when you say what you really mean, some people will think you're really mean." That's why it's important to get God's words, so that you may speak with the *"tongue of the learned"* (Isa. 50:4). There is never a need to be offensive. Yes, some people may be offended or even hurt by the truth that you will share with them. Like physical surgery, the emotional surgery caused by a confrontation is often accompanied by pain. Job declared, *"How painful are honest words!"* (Job 6:25 NIV).

Confrontation is necessary for growth. If we care, we will confront. We will risk the consequences. *"He who rebukes a man will in the end gain more favor than he who has a flattering tongue"* (Prov. 28:23 NIV).

The next time you are tempted to suffer in silence, to swallow your rage, to explode, to retreat, or to bury your head in the sand, stop and plan an effective confrontation.

Aristotle, the Greek philosopher, said, "Anyone can become angry—that is easy. But to be angry with the right person, to the right degree, at the right time, for the right purpose, and in the right way—that is not easy." I can't argue with that. I am confident, however, that *"I can do all things through Christ who strengthens me"* (Phil. 4:13). I can confront effectively without offending. *"So in everything, do to others what you would have them do to you"* (Matt. 7:12 NIV).

Endnotes

[1] Donna K. H. Walters, "Read This Story on Rudeness! Now!" *Los Angeles Times,* Sunday, 4 December 1994, Business section.

[2] Stephen R. Covey, *The Seven Habits of Highly Effective People* (New York: Simon and Schuster, 1990) p. 219.

[3] M. Scott Peck, *The Road Less Traveled* (New York: Simon and Schuster, 1979) p. 16.

Index to Biblical Conflicts